THEMES IN CANADIAN LITERATUR
General Editor *David Arnason*

The Role of Woman in Canadian Literature

Edited by
Elizabeth McCullough

Macmillan of Canada

ISBN 0-7705-1265-8

University of Regina

Themes in Canadian Literature

The Artist in Canadian Literature edited by Lionel Wilson
Canadian Humour and Satire edited by Theresa Ford
Canadian Myths and Legends edited by Michael O. Nowlan
The Depression in Canadian Literature edited by Alice K. Hale
  and Sheila Brooks
The French Canadian Experience edited by Gaston Saint-Pierre
The Frontier Experience edited by Jack Hodgins
The Immigrant Experience edited by Leuba Bailey
Isolation in Canadian Literature edited by David Arnason
The Maritime Experience edited by Michael O. Nowlan
Native Peoples in Canadian Literature edited by William and
  Christine Mowat
The Ontario Experience edited by John Stevens
The Prairie Experience edited by Terry Angus
The Role of Woman in Canadian Literature edited by Elizabeth
  McCullough
The Search for Identity edited by James Foley
The Urban Experience edited by John Stevens
The West Coast Experience edited by Jack Hodgins

Printed in Canada

ACKNOWLEDGMENTS

Grateful acknowledgment is made for the use of copyright material.

Photographs: p. 3, Joan Latchford; p. 6, Ontario Ministry of Agriculture and Food; p. 15, Miller Services Ltd.; p. 25, Ontario Ministry of Industry and Tourism; p. 52, Information Canada Photothèque; p. 65, Joan Latchford; p. 66, Canadian Press photo by Peter Bregg; p. 82, Miller Services Ltd.; p. 83, Information Canada Photothèque; p. 89, Al Beaton, *Toronto Telegram*; p. 111, Miller Services Ltd.

Doris Anderson: "Real Women in Fiction, Where Are You?" from *Chatelaine*, September 1971. Reprinted by permission of the Author.
Anonymous: "Confidences" by "A Girl of the Period", first published in *Rose Belford's Canadian Monthly*, June 1880, p. 624.
Margaret Atwood: "When you look at nothing . . ." and "It's the Story That Counts" from *You Are Happy* by Margaret Atwood, Oxford University Press, Canada, 1974. Reprinted by permission of the Author.
Marie-Claire Blais: "The Mad Woman" from *One Hundred Poems of Modern Quebec*, edited and translated by Fred Cogswell, Fiddlehead Books, New Brunswick, 1971. Reprinted by permission of Fred Cogswell.
Emily Carr: "Canoe" from *Klee Wyck* by Emily Carr, © 1941 by Clarke, Irwin & Company Limited. Used by permission.
Marian Engel: "Housework Gives Me the Crazies" from *Chatelaine*, September 1971. Reprinted by permission of the Author.
Gail Fox: "Lines in Contentment" and "Dangerous Season" from *Dangerous Season*, copyright 1969 by Gail Fox, published by Quarry Press, Kingston. Reprinted by permission of the Author.
Phyllis Gotlieb: "sometimes I think . . ." from *Doctor Umlaut's Earthly Kingdom*, copyright 1974 by Phyllis Gotlieb. Reprinted by permission of Calliope Press, Toronto.
Anne Hébert: "The Lean Girl" from *Translations of S.-D. Garneau and Anne Hébert* by F. R. Scott, Klanak Press, Vancouver (1962). Reprinted by permission of F. R. Scott.
E. Pauline Johnson: "The Grey Archway" from *Legends of Vancouver* by E. Pauline Johnson, Toronto (1911).
Judy LaMarsh: "A Woman in Politics" from *Memoirs of a Bird in a Gilded Cage* by Judy LaMarsh. Reprinted by permission of McClelland and Stewart Limited.
Margaret Laurence: "To Set Our House in Order" from *A Bird in the House* by Margaret Laurence. Reprinted by permission of McClelland and Stewart Limited, Toronto.
Dorothy Livesay: "The Unquiet Bed" and "The Three Emily's" from *The Collected Poems: The Two Seasons* by Dorothy Livesay. Reprinted by permission of McGraw-Hill Ryerson Limited.
Nellie L. McClung: "Christmas in Manitoba" from *Clearing in the West: My Own Story* by Nellie L. McClung. Reprinted by permission of Thomas Allen & Son Ltd.

Gwendolyn MacEwen: "Jewellery" and "Meditations of a Seamstress (1)" from *Armies of the Moon* by Gwendolyn MacEwen. Reprinted by permission of The Macmillan Company of Canada Limited.

Jay Macpherson: "The Gardeners" from *The Boatman and Other Poems* by Jay Macpherson. Reprinted by permission of Oxford University Press, Canada.

Claire Martin: "Springtime" from *Stories from Quebec*, edited and translated by Philip Stratford. Reprinted by permission of Van Nostrand Reinhold Ltd.

Alice Munro: "The Found Boat" from *Something I've Been Meaning to Tell You* by Alice Munro. Reprinted by permission of McGraw-Hill Ryerson Limited.

P. K. Page: "Little Girls", "Young Girls", and "Truce" from *Poems; Selected and New* by P. K. Page (1974). Reprinted by permission of the Author and The House of Anansi Press Limited.

Mary Soderstrom: "I'm Sorry Mrs. Strauss" from *Exile*, Vol. II, No. 1, 1974, published by York University. Reprinted by permission of the Author.

Audrey Thomas: "Kill Day on the Government Wharf" from *Stories from Arctic and Pacific Canada* edited by Schroeder/Wiebe, Macmillan of Canada, 1974. Reprinted by permission of George Borchardt, Inc., New York.

Catherine Parr Traill: "Gardening" from *The Female Emigrant's Guide* by Catherine Parr Traill, Toronto (1854).

Miriam Waddington: "Why Should I Care About the World" and "From a Dead Poet's Book" from *Driving Home* by Miriam Waddington. Reprinted by permission of Oxford University Press, Canada.

CONTENTS

Introduction 1

"sometimes I think . . ." *Phyllis Gotlieb* 3
Gardening *Catherine Parr Traill* 5
Why Should I Care About the World *Miriam Waddington* 7
The Grey Archway *E. Pauline Johnson* 9
From a Dead Poet's Book *Miriam Waddington* 16
Christmas in Manitoba *Nellie L. McClung* 17
"When you look at nothing . . ." *Margaret Atwood* 23
Confidences *"A Girl of the Period"* 24
The Three Emily's *Dorothy Livesay* 31
Canoe *Emily Carr* 32
The Mad Woman *Marie-Claire Blais* 35
To Set Our House in Order *Margaret Laurence* 36
Lines in Contentment *Gail Fox* 52
Dangerous Season *Gail Fox* 53
I'm Sorry Mrs. Strauss *Mary Soderstrom* 54
The Gardeners *Jay Macpherson* 60
Springtime *Claire Martin* 61
Jewellery *Gwendolyn MacEwen* 65
Real Women in Fiction, Where Are You? *Doris Anderson* 66
The Lean Girl *Anne Hébert* 69
The Found Boat *Alice Munro* 70
Little Girls *P. K. Page* 82
Young Girls *P. K. Page* 83
A Woman in Politics *Judy LaMarsh* 85
Truce *P. K. Page* 90
Housework Gives Me the Crazies *Marian Engel* 91
Meditations of a Seamstress (1) *Gwendolyn MacEwen* 102
Kill Day on the Government Wharf *Audrey Thomas* 103
The Unquiet Bed *Dorothy Livesay* 115
It's the Story That Counts *Margaret Atwood* 116

Questions on the Theme 117
Bibliography 118

INTRODUCTION

It is readily apparent that women have never suffered a lack of attention, from either male or female writers, in Canadian literature. Indeed, the task of selecting material for an anthology such as this is a pleasant one. There is such a plenitude and range of writing reflecting the experience of women in Canada that one is faced with a surfeit of riches. It is only unfortunate that, through lack of space, some fine and familiar writers about women must necessarily be left out. Susanna Moodie, L. M. Montgomery, and Ethel Wilson come to mind in this category. Nor is any slight intended to those exceptional men who have written of women with sensitivity and quite remarkable understanding — Sinclair Ross and Morley Callaghan are examples. By including only women writers, who reveal how women themselves have regarded their role, it is intended that the reader be offered an inside view, as it were, of the anthology's theme.

The writers who are represented portray a wide range of experience within the context of the nineteenth and twentieth centuries. They are concerned with being a woman, or observing other women, or creating experiences of fictional women. It should perhaps be noted that most of these writers are limited neither in subject nor in genre to what is included here. Margaret Atwood and Marian Engel are only two who write superbly in other forms, and Dorothy Livesay, for example, is more widely known for her poems about love than for the kind of artist's self-portrait in "The Three Emily's". The short bibliography included in this book suggests some of the additional worth-while writing available to the interested reader.

Because the chosen works are those of writers reflecting on intimate, often personal, experience, many of them are concerned with "small" events. From the immediate experience, however, universal expressions result. Gail Fox's response to motherhood, Dorothy Livesay's to the choice between art and family, Judy LaMarsh's to the realities of politics, speak for many women.

The selections follow the range of woman's experience from childhood through adolescence and maturity to old age. Most of them deal with women at the adolescent/young-adult stage since it is then that self-awareness and definition in terms of society are of particular interest and concern. "A Girl of the Period" and Gwendolyn MacEwen, for instance, reflect on the relationship between self and society from quite different points in time. And one can see the youthful and persistent search for self-identification in the stories by Margaret Laurence and Alice Munro. Several of the selections consider older women, particularly women artists and their work. Others assess women in social encounters and love relationships. The common denominator in all the selections is an honesty in dealing with the experience.

Not all encounters with work, society, and lovers are happy, obviously, and the loneliness and despair of the unfulfilled pervade the work of writers such as Marie-Claire Blais and Anne Hébert. The social difficulties, in particular, of being a woman, compounded as they are by the problems of being a newcomer, a member of a minority, or an individual out of step with society, are chronicled in both the poetry and the prose of women writers presented here.

The nineteenth-century material in the anthology suggests that the conflicts which we tend to consider as being of recent concern have existed for a long time. The stout feminism of Nellie McClung contrasts sharply with the orderly expectations that Mrs. Traill has of her early settlers.

As would be expected of writing that deals with such a wide range of experience, the selections also comprise a great variety of attitudes. All share realism, but the realism is variously reflected through fear, confidence, concern, tranquillity, anger, and warmth, and is sometimes sharpened with wit and irony.

It is hoped that from this sampling of the Canadian woman's view of herself over the years, from the earliest writer to the most contemporary, some idea may be gained not only of the ever-changing concept of the role of woman, but also of the importance of her continuing contribution to Canadian literature.

Elizabeth McCullough

"SOMETIMES I THINK ... "
Phyllis Gotlieb

sometimes I think the world's horizon fits
into the compass of my eye
and the rivers and the mountains and the valleys fold down
to leave the roofs and spires and sky
and there is no star
in the heavens only
a cloudy evening sky
no midnight
no daylight
but a greyblue areole wraps
the whole terrestrial sphere
except here

my old man's watching TV in the velveteen chair
with his knackers clacking in a glass of water
polishing his head because he hasn't any hair there

but I, I am the centre, I my
corona the marquee
rhinestones cover my breast and illustrate
every breath of the light, red
green yellow white
my sky of mazda stars

I'm the Dragon Priestess of Mars!!!

stepped right out of Edgar Rice Burroughs
and I've come to you you you
to set you free

so cover my hands with silver
cover my teeth with gold
and I'll take you there there
there where nobody ever grows old but me

GARDENING
Catherine Parr Traill

With a little attention and labour, the vegetable garden may be carried to great perfection by the women and children, with a little assistance from the men at the outset, in digging the ground, and securing the fences, or any work that may require strength to effect. In the new ground the surface is often encumbered with large stones, and these must either remain a blot on the fair features of the garden plot, or be rolled away by the strong arm of the men, aided by the lever. These surface stones may be made very serviceable in filling up the lower part of the fence, or, piled in large heaps, be rendered ornamental by giving them the effect of rockwork. I know many gardeners whose rustic seats, overarched by climbing plants, have been made both useful and ornamental with these blocks of granite and limestone forming the seat. Stone-crop, oprine, and many other plants, set in a little soil among the crevices, have transformed the unsightly masses into an interesting and sightly object. The Wild Cucumber, Orange Gourd, Wild Clematis, and a number of other shrubby climbing-plants, will thrive and cover the rocky pile with luxuriant foliage. Thus by the exertion of a little ingenuity, the garden of the settler may be rendered not only highly useful, but very ornamental. A little taste displayed about the rudest dwelling, will raise the inmates in the eyes of their neighbours. There are very few persons totally insensible to the enjoyment of the beautiful, either in nature or art, and still fewer who are insensible to the approbation of their fellow men; this feeling is no doubt implanted in them by the Great Creator, to encourage them in the pursuit of purer, more intellectual pleasures than belong to their grosser natures. As men cultivate the mind they rise in the scale of creation, and become more capable of adoring the Almighty through the works of His hands. —I think there can be no doubt but that whatever elevates the higher faculties of the soul, brings man a step nearer to his Maker.

How much pleasanter is the aspect of a house surrounded by

a garden, nicely weeded and kept, than the desolate chip-yard, unrelieved by any green tree or flower, that is so often seen in the new settlements in Canada. What cheerful feelings can such a barren spot excite; what home affections can it nourish in the heart of the emigrant wife? Even though she may have to labour to rear it with her own hands, let her plant a garden.

WHY SHOULD I CARE ABOUT THE WORLD
Miriam Waddington

Gone is
the holiness
in where I
lived, my song.

Why should I care
what happens to
the world why
should I
broodingly
seek the cell of
holiness the
habit in where
I lived, my song?

(Your song
was only a few
ragged Scotsmen
in Kildonan, some
riff-raffy settlers,
half-breeds, Indians,
Galician labourers,
scraggly-ended
pee-smelling prairie
towns)

(it was a flat
stony mound
for a mountain
a silly tuft
of pine on
an island in
Lac du Bonnet,
berry-picking in a
buffalo summer

beside a wheat ocean
and jumping the
ditches brimming
with rain.)

Gone now; all
cracked open like
eggs at Easter
parted like three
feathers in a
bird's tail of wind.

And I can't even
go back to being
dirty Jew, to
hearing from the
conductor on the
Selkirk streetcar:
*your father is
a Bolshevik isn't
he little girl?*

This is a very
far very long
way to be away
from the holiness
in where I lived
my song.

THE GREY ARCHWAY
E. Pauline Johnson

The steamer, like a huge shuttle, wove in and out among the countless small islands; its long trailing scarf of grey smoke hung heavily along the uncertain shores, casting a shadow over the pearly waters of the Pacific, which swung lazily from rock to rock in indescribable beauty.

After dinner I wandered astern with the traveller's ever-present hope of seeing the beauties of a typical Northern sunset, and by some happy chance I placed my deck stool near an old tillicum, who was leaning on the rail, his pipe between his thin curved lips, his brown hands clasped idly, his sombre eyes looking far out to sea, as though they searched the future — or was it that they were seeing the past?

"Kla-how-ya, tillicum!" I greeted.

He glanced round, and half smiled.

"Kla-how-ya, tillicum!" he replied, with the warmth of friendliness I have always met with among the Pacific tribes.

I drew my deck stool nearer to him, and he acknowledged the action with another half-smile, but did not stir from his entrenchment, remaining as if hedged about with an inviolable fortress of exclusiveness. Yet I knew that my Chinook salutation would be a draw-bridge by which I might hope to cross the moat into his castle of silence.

Indian-like, he took his time before continuing the acquaintance. Then he began in most excellent English:

"You do not know these Northern waters?"

I shook my head.

After many moments he leaned forwards, looking along the curve of the deck, up the channels and narrows we were threading, to a broad strip of waters off the port bow. Then he pointed with that peculiar, thoroughly Indian gesture of the palm uppermost.

"Do you see it — over there? The small island? It rests on the edge of the water, like a grey gull."

It took my unaccustomed eyes some moments to discern it;

9

then all at once I caught its outline, veiled in the mists of distance — grey, cobwebby, dreamy.

"Yes," I replied, "I see it now. You will tell me of it — tillicum?"

He gave a swift glance at my dark skin, then nodded. "You are one of us," he said, with evidently no thought of a possible contradiction. "And you will understand, or I should not tell you. You will not smile at the story, for you are one of us."

"I am one of you, and I shall understand," I answered.

It was a full half-hour before we neared the island, yet neither of us spoke during that time; then, as the "grey gull" shaped itself into rock and tree and crag, I noticed in the very centre a stupendous pile of stone lifting itself skyward, without fissure or cleft; but a peculiar haziness about the base made me peer narrowly to catch the perfect outline.

"It is the 'Grey Archway'," he explained simply.

Only then did I grasp the singular formation before us; the rock itself was a perfect archway, through which we could see the placid Pacific shimmering in the growing colours of the coming sunset at the opposite rim of the island.

"What a remarkable whim of Nature!" I exclaimed, but his brown hand was laid in a contradictory grasp on my arm, and he snatched up my comment almost with impatience.

"No, it was not Nature," he said. "That is the reason I say you will understand — you are one of us — you will know what I tell you is true. The Great Tyee did not make that archway, it was — " here his voice lowered — "it was magic, red man's medicine and magic — you savvy?"

"Yes," I said. "Tell me, for I — savvy."

"Long time ago," he began, stumbling into a half-broken English language because, I think, of the atmosphere and environment, "long before you were born, or your father, or grandfather, or even his father, this strange thing happened. It is a story for women to hear, to remember. Women are the future mothers of the tribe, and we of the Pacific Coast hold

10

such in high regard, in great reverence. The women who are mothers — o-ho! — they are the important ones, we say. Warriors, fighters, brave men, fearless daughters, owe their qualities to these mothers — eh, is it not always so?"

I nodded silently. The island was swinging nearer to us, the "Grey Archway" loomed almost above us, the mysticism crowded close, it enveloped me, caressed me, appealed to me.

"And?" I hinted.

"And," he proceeded, "this 'Grey Archway' is a story of mothers, of magic, of witchcraft, of warriors, of — love."

An Indian rarely uses the word "love", and when he does it expresses every quality, every attribute, every intensity, emotion, and passion embraced in those four little letters. Surely this was an exceptional story I was to hear.

I did not answer, only looked across the pulsing waters towards the "Grey Archway", which the sinking sun was touching with soft pastels, tints one could give no name to, beauties impossible to describe.

"You have not heard of Yaada?" he questioned. Then fortunately he continued without waiting for a reply. He well knew that I had never heard of Yaada, so why not begin without preliminary to tell me of her? — so —

"Yaada was the loveliest daughter of the Haida tribe. Young braves from all the islands, from the mainland, from the upper Skeena country came, hoping to carry her to their far-off lodges, but they always returned alone. She was the most desired of all the island maidens, beautiful, brave, modest, the daughter of her own mother.

"But there was a great man, a very great man — a medicine man, skilful, powerful, influential, old, deplorably old, and very, very rich; he said, 'Yaada shall be my wife.' And there was a young fisherman, handsome, loyal, boyish, poor, oh! very poor, and gloriously young, and he, too, said, 'Yaada shall be my wife.'

"But Yaada's mother sat apart and thought and dreamed, as mothers will. She said to herself, 'The great medicine man has

11

power, has vast riches, and wonderful magic, why not give her to him? But Ulka has the boy's heart, the boy's beauty, he is very brave, very strong; why not give her to him?'

"But the laws of the great Haida tribe prevailed. Its wise men said, 'Give the girl to the greatest man, give her to the most powerful, the richest. The man of magic must have his choice.'

"But at this the mother's heart grew as wax in the summer sunshine — it is a strange quality that mothers' hearts are made of! 'Give her to the best man — the man her heart holds highest,' said this Haida mother.

"Then Yaada spoke: 'I am the daughter of my tribe; I would judge of men by their excellence. He who proves most worthy I shall marry; it is not riches that make a good husband; it is not beauty that makes a good father for one's children. Let me and my tribe see some proof of the excellence of these two men — then, only, shall I choose who is to be the father of my children. Let us have a trial of their skill; let them show me how evil or how beautiful is the inside of their hearts. Let each of them throw a stone with some intent, some purpose in their hearts. He who makes the noblest mark may call me wife.'

"'Alas! Alas!' wailed the Haida mother. 'This casting of stones does not show worth. It but shows prowess.'

"'But I have implored the Sagalie Tyee of my father, and of his fathers before him, to help me to judge between them by this means,' said the girl. 'So they must cast the stones. In this way only shall I see their innermost hearts.'

"The medicine man never looked so old as at that moment; so hopelessly old, so wrinkled, so palsied: he was no mate for Yaada. Ulka never looked so god-like in his young beauty, so gloriously young, so courageous. The girl, looking at him, loved him — almost was she placing her hand in his, but the spirit of her forefathers halted her. She had spoken the word — she must abide by it. 'Throw!' she commanded.

"Into his shrivelled fingers the great medicine man took a

12

small, round stone, chanting strange words of magic all the while; his greedy eyes were on the girl, his greedy thoughts about her.

"Into his strong, young fingers Ulka took a smooth, flat stone; his handsome eyes were lowered in boyish modesty, his thoughts were worshipping her. The great medicine man cast his missile first; it swept through the air like a shaft of lightning, striking the great rock with a force that shattered it. At the touch of that stone the 'Grey Archway' opened and has remained open to this day.

"'Oh, wonderful power and magic!' clamoured the entire tribe. 'The very rocks do his bidding.'

"But Yaada stood with eyes that burned in agony. Ulka could never command such magic — she knew it. At her side Ulka was standing erect, tall, slender, and beautiful, but just as he cast his missile the evil voice of the old medicine man began a still more evil incantation. He fixed his poisonous eyes on the younger man, eyes with hideous magic in their depths — ill-omened and enchanted with 'bad medicine'. The stone left Ulka's fingers; for a second it flew forth in a straight line, then as the evil voice of the old man grew louder in its incantations the stone curved. Magic had waylaid the strong arm of the young brave. The stone poised an instant above the forehead of Yaada's mother, then dropped with the weight of many mountains, and the last long sleep fell upon her.

"'Slayer of my mother,' stormed the girl, her suffering eyes fixed upon the medicine man. 'Oh, I now see your black heart through your black magic. Through good magic you cut the 'Grey Archway', but your evil magic you used upon young Ulka. I saw your wicked eyes upon him; I heard your wicked incantations; I know your wicked heart. You used your heartless magic in hope of winning me — in hope of making him an outcast of the tribe. You cared not for my sorrowing heart, my motherless life to come.' Then turning to the tribe, she demanded: 'Who of you saw his evil eyes fixed on Ulka? Who of you heard his evil song?'"

"'I,' and 'I,' and 'I,' came voice after voice.

"'The very air is poisoned that we breathe about him,' they shouted. 'The young man is blameless, his heart is as the sun, but the man who has used his evil magic has a heart black and cold as the hours before the dawn.'

"Then Yaada's voice arose in a strange, sweet, sorrowful chant:

> *My feet shall walk no more upon this island,*
> *With its great, Grey Archway.*
> *My mother sleeps forever on this island,*
> *With its great, Grey Archway.*
> *My heart would break without her on this island,*
> *With its great, Grey Archway.*
> *My life was of her life upon this island,*
> *With its great, Grey Archway.*
> *My mother's soul has wandered from this island,*
> *With its great, Grey Archway.*
> *My feet must follow hers beyond this island,*
> *With its great, Grey Archway.*

"As Yaada chanted and wailed her farewell, she moved slowly towards the edge of the cliff. On its brink she hovered a moment with outstretched arms, as a sea gull poises on its weight — then she called:

"'Ulka, my Ulka! Your hand is innocent of wrong; it was the evil magic of your rival that slew my mother. I must go to her; even you cannot keep me here; will you stay, or come with me? Oh! my Ulka!'

"The slender, gloriously young boy sprang towards her; their hands closed one within the other; for a second they poised on the brink of the rocks, radiant as stars; then together they plunged into the sea."

The legend was ended. Long ago we had passed the island with its "Grey Archway"; it was melting into the twilight, far astern.

14

As I brooded over this strange tale of a daughter's devotion, I watched the sea and sky for something that would give me a clue to the inevitable sequel that the tillicum, like all his race, was surely withholding until the opportune moment.

Something flashed through the darkening waters not a stone's throw from the steamer. I leaned forwards, watching it intently. Two silvery fish were making a succession of little leaps and plunges along the surface of the sea, their bodies catching the last tints of sunset, like flashing jewels. I looked at the tillicum quickly. He was watching me — a world of anxiety in his half-mournful eyes.

"And those two silvery fish?" I questioned.

He smiled. The anxious look vanished. "I was right," he said; "you do know us and our ways, for you are one of us. Yes, those fish are seen only in these waters; there are never but two of them. They are Yaada and her mate seeking for the soul of the Haida woman — her mother."

FROM A DEAD POET'S BOOK
Miriam Waddington

There was the sound
of your breathing
and your voice
saying *forever*
a word from a line
in a dead poet's book.

There was light
from a candle
there was a wall
and a forest and
darkness an island
with yourself

and myself floating
from sleep we
watched last autumn's
love apples fanning
and tossing on seas
in the darkness

and through darkness
and light felt
snow on the rooftops
in a distant city in
a lonely nightwatch;
there was a sound

of your breathing,
like a burning garland
forever hung above us,
winter burned, apples
glittered and words
froze on the branches;

and everywhere in
darkness was *forever*
and everywhere in
darkness was your
voice and everywhere
the distant city and
everywhere (I almost
said) everywhere was
my love

CHRISTMAS IN MANITOBA
Nellie L. McClung

Christmas Day has always been flavored to me with the pound cake and apple-jelly tarts of those first days in Manitoba.

The front-room always got a new coat of white-wash on the log walls at Christmas, and everything was scoured as white as sand or soap could make it. The hand-knit lace curtains, brought from Ontario, were washed and starched and stretched on home-made frames, so they would hang straight and reach the floor. Short curtains were considered slightly indecent. The two long widths of rag carpet in bright stripes with orange warp were brought out and laid on the white floor, with the good mats, one hooked and one braided. The homemade lounge had a covering of dark maroon canton flannel and was well supplied with patch-work cushions, crazy pattern of silks and satins and two log cabins, one made of "stuff pieces", the other one of prints. There were two bookcases made with spools, painted black, and set with shelves and a "what-not" of five shelves, on which stood china ornaments, a shell box, with a green plush pin-cushion on the top, apples filled with cloves, and cups and saucers (honorably retired from active service because of cracks, or missing handles, but with these defects tactfully concealed in the way they were placed), colored glass mugs, and on the top, a bouquet of prairie grasses, set in a frosted glass vase, a lace pattern on deep blue. I remember it well, for I broke it years later, when bouncing a ball, on the floor. Who would have thought a yarn ball would bounce so high?

When the weather got cold, the kitchen stove had to be brought into the big room, and it was a family grief when this change had to be made. If the weather did not come down too hard, the stove was kept out until after Christmas. Later when the storm doors and windows were added, and a bigger heater bought, a fine big barrel of a stove, with a row of mica windows around its middle, through which the coals glowed with all the colors of a sunset, the kitchen stove remained in the kitchen all winter.

But even when the kitchen stove was in the middle of the big room, there was a cheerful roominess about it. The wood-box papered with pictures of the Ice Palace, in Montreal (*Family Herald Supplement*), when covered with two boards over which a quilt was spread made a nice warm seat and when we got the hanging lamp from Brandon, with a pale pink shade, on which a brown deer poised for a leap across a chasm, through which a green stream dashed in foam on the rocks, the effect was magical and in the pink light the white-washed walls were softened into alabaster.

We had two new pictures now, enlarged photographs of father and mother in heavy oak frames with a gilt edge, done by a travelling artist, who drove a team of mules and carried a few lines of tinware. Every family in the neighbourhood had taken advantage of his easy plan to secure a lasting work of art. You paid only for the frame and received the picture entirely free though this offer might be withdrawn any minute for he was doing this merely to get his work known. He said there was no nicer way to give one's parents a pleasant surprise, and the pictures would be delivered in time for Christmas. When they came, we all had a surprise. We had thought that the seven dollars and thirty-five cents paid for both frames but we were wrong. Each one cost that amount and even at that the artist was losing money. The pictures were accepted and hung on the log walls, and in the declivities behind them were kept tissue paper patterns, news-paper clippings, and other semi-precious documents, thus relieving the congestion in the real archives, lodged in the lower regions of the clock, where notes, grain-tickets, tax receipts were kept.

After the Christmas dinner of turkey and plum pudding, the men sat and talked of the trouble Louis Riel was causing. He had come back from Montana, where he had been teaching school, and was now in Saskatchewan, stirring up the half-breeds and Indians and inciting them to make raids on the white settlers.

"Why don't they arrest him now, and get him safely in jail before someone is killed?" Mother was greatly disturbed over the situation. "I can't sleep," she said, "thinking of the poor women there, frightened to go to sleep at night. They say he has given guns to the Indians and there will be another massacre like there was in Minnesota."

Frank Burnett was indignant that the Government had not sent an armed force, just as soon as the trouble began.

"Uniforms would settle the trouble," he said; "the red coats and the flash of steel, a few guns fired and the half-breeds and Indians would know there was law in the country. Riel should be hanged anyway for the murder of Thos. Scott."

I wanted to talk. Mr. Schultz had told us about it in school. The half-breeds and Indians had a grievance, a real one. The settlers were crowding in on them, their land was being surveyed over again, and divided into squares like ours. They had long narrow lots, as they had along the Red and Assiniboine, so they could live side by side, and now a new arrangement of land was being made and they were afraid their land was going to be taken from them. When they sent letters to Ottawa, they got no replies.

I knew how they felt. I had often asked for explanations and got the prescribed 19th century dusty answer, "because I say so — that's all the reason you need." How I hated it! And how unfair I felt it to be! The Government officials were treating the Indians the same way.

I knew the government was to blame but I would not be allowed to say it, and if I did get it said, I might get Mr. Schultz into trouble. Mother would feel he was undermining our respect for authority.

But much to my delight, Hannah came forward and defended the half-breeds. Hannah was always listened to when she spoke. She had what I lacked, a quiet and dignified way of expression.

"The country belonged to the Indians and half-breeds," she said in her even voice. "We must not forget that. I know they have made little use of it and must yield it to white settlers, in time, but there's enough territory for everyone if it is handled right, and they could be easily appeased and satisfied."

She told about the new survey, about the delay in getting the patents out for the land the half-breeds had proved-up on, about the slaughter of the buffalo, the Indians' source of food and clothing.

Hannah was fifteen then, with a fine presence, fair skin, a round face, and fine large greenish-blue eyes, and abundant bright brown hair, inclined to curl. She had been wiping dishes behind the stove and came out with a plate in one hand, and a flour-sack tea towel in the other. Her face was flushed and her eyes bright and to me she looked like Joan of Arc. I was very proud of her, but I knew there was a sudden tightening of the atmosphere. Even now, men do not like to be taught by women, but at that time for a girl of fifteen to presume to have an opinion, was against all tradition. However, Hannah had a prestige all her own.

She went on. "It is not the Catholic church, and it is not Louis Riel, who is causing the trouble — it is the stupidity of the Government at Ottawa, and if settlers are killed by the Indians theirs will be the guilt. A few words of explanation, a few concessions and peace could be restored."

"My God!" exclaimed Frank Burnett in real concern, "that's hot talk, Hannah, you've said enough to hang you in some countries. If you were in Russia, you would be shot for a Nihilist, my girl."

My mother was too much amazed to speak. If I had said half of what Hannah had, she would know what to do with me, but Hannah, quiet, dignified Hannah, the image of her own mother, Margaret Fullerton McCurdy, could not be sent upstairs in disgrace.

Hannah went on wiping the dishes with great composure. She had said what she wanted to say and now withdrew from the conversation. Her hearers had heard the truth, and they could take it or leave it. Responsibility had passed from her to them.

20

Mr. Burnett continued the argument. "I am afraid there is bad work going on at Northfield School," he said. "I gather that is where Hannah gets her ideas. This man Schultz is a German; he has no love for British institutions and is using his position as a teacher to undermine the children's respect for authority. We'll have to look into this. We'll have to call a meeting of the trustees."

My heart stood still. Had we involved our teacher in some trouble that might lead to his losing a job?

They all began to talk; and I could feel a hostile tide of opinion gathering and sweeping ahead of it all good sense and reason and it seemed to me I would have to speak, no matter what happened. Will would listen to me anyway. I went over and stood before him.

"Will," I said, "I want to talk, make them keep quiet."

"Nellie has something on her mind," Will called out in his good humoured way. "It is not often this poor tongue-tied child wants to talk, and she should get her chance on Christmas day, of all times."

Mother rose up to protest, but Will waved her back.

"Let the kid talk," he said, "talk won't hurt anyone. It's the things we don't say that hurt us, I know."

Then came the ordeal, when the silence fell on the room. I have faced audiences who were hostile since then and encountered unfriendly glances, but the antagonism here was more terrible, being directed, not as much against what I had to say, as against the fact that I dared to say anything.

I addressed Will, as people air their views in letters addressed to the Editor. "The Government is like the Machine Company, Will," I said. "The half-breeds are dissatisfied with the way they are treated, they are afraid they are going to be put off their farms, just as we were afraid when the tongue of the binder broke, and we saw we were going to lose our crop. The half-breeds have written letters, and sent people to see the Government and asked them to send out someone to straighten out their troubles, just as you, Will, wrote letters

21

to the Company and asked them to send an expert, who would put the binder in good shape. The Government won't answer the half-breeds, won't notice them, won't talk to them — and the only word they send them is a saucy word — 'what we will send you will be an army; we'll put you in your place.' Just as the Machine Company wrote us a saucy letter saying that it was our own fault if the binders broke, and they couldn't supply us with brains. It's the same spirit. We should understand how the half-breeds feel. That's all I want to say," and before anyone could say a word, I left the room, glad to get away.

"WHEN YOU LOOK AT NOTHING . . . "
Margaret Atwood

When you look at nothing
what are you looking at?
Whose face floats on the water
dissolving like a paper plate?

It's the first one, remember,
the one you thought you abandoned
along with the furniture.

You returned to her after the other war
and look what happened.
Now you are wondering
whether to do it again.

Meanwhile she sits in her chair
waxing and waning
like an inner tube or a mother,
breathing out, breathing in,

surrounded by bowls, bowls, bowls,
tributes from the suitors
who are having a good time in the kitchen

waiting for her to decide
on the dialogue for this evening
which will be in perfect taste
and will include tea and sex
dispensed graciously both at once.

She's up to something, she's weaving
histories, they are never right,
she has to do them over,
she is weaving her version,

the one you will believe in,
the only one you will hear.

CONFIDENCES
"A Girl of the Period"

From *Rose Belford's Canadian Monthly*, June, 1880.

In these days of "women's rights" and even "children's rights" I feel hopeful a little that there may be some chance for a "girl of the period" to state what she thinks about her wrongs in the pages of such an "advanced" publication as the *Canadian Monthly* justly claims to be. I don't care what row people make about it; for you'll keep my secret — won't you? Mr. Editor — and not let anybody know who your contributor is.

"I want to know why" about a lot of things; and I don't care if some of your smart contributors think me a "dreadful stupid" if only they will really deluge me with their wisdom.

I want to know why it is that I, a well brought-up lady-like (excuse my self-conceit — but this is the remark people make of me) girl, am so utterly helpless and dependent. I have not been taught anything that is of the slightest earthly use to anybody in the whole world. Of course I can sing correctly; but have no special power or compass of voice. It is only soft and low — a peculiarity of voice which Milton (?), or some of these old poets, says is nice in a woman, because it keeps her from scolding, I suppose. As a pianist I am a *brilliant success,* and yet a humbug as regards the science of music. That goes without saying. I can waltz — well! "divinely" — but no thanks to anybody for that; it comes *con amore*; I can sew — fancy work; but I could not cut out and "build" a dress, even if I was never to have another. I can't make up a bonnet, nor even a hat; but I *do* know when the milliner has made a mess of either. I am self-conceited enough to think I have extremely good taste in such matters as a critic, yet I don't see how I could turn my good taste into a single solitary dollar if I had to. I just love parties, balls, concerts and — shall I confess it? — theatres, and yet, if I had to earn the money with which to gratify myself in these indulgences, I fancy I must perforce go amusementless for many a year. My dear old "Pater" and my good kind mamma are fairly well-off, I believe (but I really don't know), and are very willing to give me a good share of

all these enjoyments; but it does make me often "feel mean" to know that I am utterly dependent on them for everything, and can't do anything to lighten their load. Why mamma won't even let me into the kitchen to learn how to do things. She says it is not lady-like.

A girl not out of her "teens" yet can't be expected, perhaps, to have much brains, and so it puzzles me awfully to understand why it should be, that my brother Jack, aged sixteen, and Bill, aged twenty-two, both work, the one as an office boy in a warehouse (he calls it sub-book-keeper), the other as traveller for a wholesale grocery house, and yet both are looked upon as quite respectable. Bill is asked out to all the parties with me. But if I, a girl, as Bill tries with much pains and wealth of oratory to explain to me, were known to work, *everybody* would "cut" me at once; I would be just "a work-girl, you see," he says conclusively, as though that were any solution of the question or settled it at all. Why do not the smell of sugar and the raisin and molasses spots which adhere to the nether and upper integuments of his working apparel adhere also socially to his full dress suit when he dons it? It is a conundrum, and I give it up; just as completely as I give up the other conundrum of why it should be that similar spots on a working suit of mine should inevitably reveal themselves socially, as he says they would, on any party dress I might don, however "swell" it might be? I try to argue the thing out on this line with Bill sometimes, but he only gets mad; says girls don't know anything and can't be rational for five consecutive minutes, and goes off fuming with some favourite quotation of his from some nasty old philosopher, about "women being unreasoning animals that poke the fire from the top" or light stoves with coal oil, &c., &c.

But I vow and declare I can't see that I am so irrational. Why should I have been so fettered and useless? My mother only laughs when I torment her about it and tells me I'll soon drop all that nonsense when I get "engaged" to some gentlemanly young fellow; but that interesting youth is hard to find, and when something that looks like him does turn up it invariably becomes painfully evident that it would be a shame to add to the burdens already laid upon his slender income by "society" and social requirements. In fact I am shut up to a choice of ungentlemanly young men, who are half-old and so wholly coarse or self-conceited through having "fought their way up from the ranks" as papa puts it, that one can't help wishing they had stayed in those "ranks" they are so eminently fitted to adorn.

It is towards one of these useful, practical, self-raised men, that poor useless me is hintingly thrust by anxious relatives both near and distant. His usefulness is supposed to be eminently adapted to my uselessness. He, the self-raised one, is expected to raze me down to his level. I confess I don't like the prospect; and I'm not so sure that Jones does either (his name is Jones — *Mrs.* Jones, fancy!!!). He and I have not a solitary taste in common. So, in self-defence, I take broad hints regarding my probable future destiny as mild attempts at jocularity, and vent my pent-up indignation on my long-suffering relatives in wicked conundrums and other pleasantries at the expense of my would-be husband; but nobody sympathizes with these sallies except my good old papa. He laughs, and is severely rebuked for encouraging my folly. But with that moral support — highly moral I think — I am too much for my disinterested relatives. I don't "make eyes" at Jones. He is getting discouraged. My relatives begin to look upon him (and me) as lost.

I feel lost a little myself too — lost, useless, and mean — to think that I only dawdle around and can only look pretty — that is as pretty as I can, you know. I eat up, dress up, and spend the "proceeds" — that's a business word, isn't it? — of the labours of others without being a bit the happier for it.

And then there's another side to it, too, which I can't talk much about to sympathizing (?) relatives; but I will to you, dear Public, because some of you may be "girls of the period" like me and will understand. There are nights when I am peculiarly disgusted with myself, and I sit up and moon and cry my eyes out, because — well because I am miserable and feel such a little fool. For visions of Charlie — Charlie Rivers — will intrude at such times. He is so nice. He's simply splendid! Of course, I don't *care* for him particularly; but then I think if I tried hard I might get almost to like him. I think, and think, and think. He's a clerk you know, and papa says has got six hundred or eight hundred dollars — somewhere about that a year. But whatever his salary, he keeps himself quite like a gentleman. He's a great flirt they say, but he doesn't *ever* flirt with me. He and I always talk quite seriously. He says he lives in "diggings", and describes the royal times he has roughing it all by himself in a "growlery" of his own; informs me what a splendid cook he is, and that he has learned it all by the light of nature. But then papa says "he'll never be anything. He's not sharp and has queer ideas — a good fellow, but a *soft*." I think I know what he means by that, because Charlie talks to me sometimes — on the stairs at parties you know — like this, with an odd, puzzled, weary look in his eyes. "I am worried, Miss Kate, I know I'll never be rich. I can't see my way to do the mean things necessary to get on. Not but what I am content enough to do so much work — good work, the best I've got in me — for so much pay all my life. But then if a fellow were to fall in love — get tumbled right into it before he knew — what is he to do about it? Is he to keep to his principles and lose his love, or is he to lose his principles, go in wild for money, gain his loved one, lose his own respect, and risk the loss of hers when she finds out what a mean money-grubbing wretch he has become in order to get her? That is *the* conundrum to me, Miss Kate. Have you any answer to it?" And then he looks, oh! so anxious and troubled that — I have to ask him to button my glove for me, just to change the subject. But it does not do it always. During the buttoning process he looks awfully solemn, says it's a shame to bother me about his little troubles, and that he won't fall in love at all if I don't want him to, &c., &c., till I don't know what to say, and he proposes — another waltz.

Why, oh! why, dear Public, should I need to be dumb? What have I done, or not done, that I should have no experience of real life such as he has, and so be unable to give him sound and rational advice?

Just at present the moon is full, and moonstruck visions assail me. How thoroughly jolly it would be if girls like myself were brought up to some form of trade, profession, or business, so that, when we come of age, we might earn enough to suffice for our real needs. These needs are not so very great after all; only neat, pretty, but not ever-varying and fanciful dress, and food and shelter. Steady, necessitated occupation would be a real blessing to most of us, and then if we did meet the awful fate portrayed by Charlie, and tumbled headlong into love, why we needn't be the least bit of a burden to the other "tumbler" when we both came to the

28

surface again, but might swim to shore hand in hand. Two eight hundred dollars a year to support two "diggingses" rolled into *one,* might surely make that *one* extra cosy and comfortable, mightn't it? and neither of us need then be a bit more mean or money-grubbing than before. If each unit (scientific word, isn't it?) could maintain itself apart, would it be any more, or any less, difficult when united?

There are such heaps and heaps of things women might do if anybody would show them how. Why, the Kindergarten system alone is quite a mine of wealth and of work to us, and might be extended indefinitely down to the very babies. Some of the married women, as well as the single, could attend to that, while others of the married ones who had children of their own, could leave their children at the Kindergarten during the day, and pursue other forms of labour themselves. Very pretty pictures are made of the husband and father wending his way home in the cool of the evening, certain of welcome from his loved ones. Why does no one sketch the wife and mother strolling home from her toil on the arm of her husband to their mutual home, alike joyous in anticipation of shouts of welcome, clinging kisses and sweet caresses from their little ones, just returned from the Kindergarten? Why may not such elements of happiness constitute a happy home for each and all; Father, Mother, and children? Each, with the experiences of the day spent in different ways, amid different scenes, can pour these into willing ears. Each can gladden each with the restful sympathy and endearment of true home love; all the more dear for the brief daily separation.

Probably the moon's influence, if turned strongly in such a direction, would upset the existing order of things a good deal in this mad world, and cause a tide in the affairs of men strong enough to sweep through a lot of social barriers of the pitchfork kind, but what of that? There are many things social which need upsetting badly, and although I am only "a girl of the period", and don't know much, I *do* know this, that the more the work of the world is wisely shared among all its

29

denizens, both men and women, the less strain there will be on each to satisfy purely natural wants. And so it might come yet to be as possible for a woman, as for a man, to do the share of the world's work which is properly hers, and yet live her special *rôle* in life out of its completeness, if her work were subdivided and systematized as man's is.

But the moon is drawing me a little out of my depth. I must not be caught and swept away by her tide.

It's all that horrid Charlie. His worried look haunts me continually. Not that I am smitten with him at all. You must not think that, and of course his name isn't "Charlie", nor mine "Kate". But I can't help thinking often that if the world were different, so that I would not need thereby to cast such a moral and physical burden on him, I might be tempted to take a kind of interest in *him* as well as in the wrongs and woes, the rights and uses, of we poor "girls of the period". As it is, how can any girl who truly loves someone whom she also admires and respects, far more than she does herself, consider it a proof of real love to put such a fearful burden upon him as is meant by that peculiar and entirely abnormal development of this nineteenth century called

"A Girl of the Period"?

THE THREE EMILY'S*
Dorothy Livesay

These women crying in my head
Walk alone, uncomforted:
The Emily's, these three
Cry to be set free —
And others whom I will not name
Each different, each the same.

Yet they had liberty!
Their kingdom was the sky:
They batted clouds with easy hand,
Found a mountain for their stand;
From wandering lonely they could catch
The inner magic of a heath —
A lake their palette, any tree
Their brush could be.

And still they cry to me
As in reproach —
I, born to hear their inner storm
Of separate man in woman's form,
I yet possess another kingdom, barred
To them, these three, this Emily.
I move as mother in a frame,
My arteries
Flow the immemorial way
Towards the child, the man;
And only for brief span
Am I an Emily on mountain snows
And one of these.

And so the whole that I possess
Is still much less —
They move triumphant through my head:
I am the one
Uncomforted.

*Emily Brontë, Emily Dickinson, and Emily Carr

31

CANOE
Emily Carr

Three red bulls — sluggish bestial creatures with white faces and morose bloodshot eyes — made me long to get away from the village. But I could not: there was no boat.

I knew the roof and the ricketiness of every Indian woodshed. This was the steepest roof of them all, and I was panting a bit. It is not easy to climb with a little dog in one hand and the hot breath of three bulls close behind you. Those three detestable white faces were clustered round my canvas below. They were giving terrible bellows and hoofing up the sand.

Far across the water there appeared a tiny speck: it grew and grew. By the time the bulls had decided to move on, it was a sizeable canoe heading for the mud-flats beyond the beach. The tide was very far out. When the canoe grounded down there on the mud, an Indian family swarmed over her side, and began plodding heavily across the sucking ooze towards an Indian hut above the beach. I met them where the sand and the mud joined.

"Are you going back to Alliford? Will you take me?"

"Uh huh," they were; "Uh huh," they would.

"How soon?"

"Plitty-big-hully-up-quick."

I ran up the hill to the mission house. Lunch was ready but I did not wait. I packed my things in a hurry and ran down the hill to the Indian hut, and sat myself on a beach log where I could watch the Indians' movements.

The Indians gathered raspberries from a poor little patch at the back of the house. They borrowed a huge preserving kettle from the farthest house in the village. Grandpa fetched it; his locomotion was very slow. The women took pails to the village tap, lit a fire, heated water; washed clothes — hung out — gathered in; set dough, made bread, baked bread; boiled jam, bottled jam; cooked meals and ate meals. Grandpa and the baby took sleeps on the kitchen floor, while I sat and sat on my log with my little dog in my lap, waiting. When the bulls came down our way I ran, clutching the dog. When the bulls had passed, we sat down again. But even when I was running, I watched the canoe. Sometimes I went to the door and asked,

"When do we go?"

"Bymby," or "Plitty soon," they said.

I suggested going up to the mission house to get something to eat, but they shook their heads violently, made the motion of swift running in the direction of the canoe and said, "Big-hully-up-quick."

I found a ship's biscuit and a wizened apple in my sketch sack. They smelled of turpentine and revolted my appetite. At dusk I ate them greedily.

It did not get dark. The sun and moon crossed ways before day ended. By and by the bulls nodded up the hill and sat in front of the mission gate to spend the night. In the house the Indians lit a coal-oil lamp. The tide brought the canoe in. She floated there before me.

At nine o'clock everything was ready. The Indians waded back and forth stowing the jam, the hot bread, the wash, and sundry bundles in the canoe. They beckoned to me. As I waded out, the water was icy against my naked feet. I was given the bow seat, a small round stick like a hen roost. I sat down on the floor and rested my back against the roost, holding the small dog in my lap. Behind me in the point of the canoe were two Indian dogs, which kept thrusting mangy muzzles under my arms, sniffing at my griffon dog.

Grandpa took one oar, the small boy of six the other. The mother in the stern held a sleeping child under her shawl and grasped the steering paddle. A young girl beside her settled into a shawl-swathed hump. Children tumbled themselves among the household goods and immediately slept.

Loosed from her mooring, the big canoe glided forward. The man and the boy rowed her into the current. When she met it she swerved like a frightened horse — accepted — gave herself to its guiding, her wolf's head stuck proud and high above the water.

The child-rower tipped forward in sleep and rolled among the bundles. The old man, shipping the child's oar and his own, slumped down among the jam, loaves and washing, resting his bent old back against the thwart.

The canoe passed shores crammed with trees — trees overhanging stony beaches, trees held back by rocky cliffs, pointed fir trees climbing in dark masses up the mountain sides, moonlight silvering their blackness.

Our going was imperceptible, the woman's steering paddle the only thing that moved, its silent cuts stirring phosporus like white fire.

Time and texture faded . . . ceased to exist . . . day was gone, yet it was not night. Water was not wet nor deep, just smoothness spread with light.

As the canoe glided on, her human cargo was as silent as the cedar-life that once had filled her. She had done with the forest now; when they shoved her into the sea they had dug out her heart. Submissively she accepted the new element, going with the tide. When tide or wind crossed her she became fractious. Some still element of the forest clung yet to the cedar's hollow rind which resented the restless push of waves.

Once only during the whole trip were words exchanged in the canoe. The old man, turning to me, said, "Where you come from?"

"Victoria."

"Victorlia? Victorlia good place — still. Vancouver, Seattle, lots, lots trouble. Victorlia plenty still."

It was midnight when the wolf-like nose of our canoe nuzzled up to the landing at Alliford. All the village was dark. Our little group was silhouetted on the landing for one moment while silver passed from my hand to the Indian's.

"Good-night."

"Gu-ni'."

One solitary speck and a huddle of specks moved across the beach, crossed the edge of visibility and plunged into immense night.

Slowly the canoe drifted away from the moonlit landing, till, at the end of her rope, she lay an empty thing, floating among the shadows of an inverted forest.

34

THE MAD WOMAN
Marie-Claire Blais

(Translated by Fred Cogswell)

They put her a little out of the way
In the humid and pleasant confusion
Of a Winter house,
She is not sad
Near the plants and roses,

Do not believe that she cries . . .

Gently, she rests
In a languishing forest on the threshold of the world
Her face is at rest
Under the murmuring and warm leaves
That make a crown for it,
She is scarcely sleeping, she still breathes
Fine springs run between her drowsy lips,
She calls out sometimes
When she hears footsteps
Then forgets just as quickly
Among the roses and plants . . .

TO SET OUR HOUSE IN ORDER
Margaret Laurence

When the baby was almost ready to be born, something went
wrong and my mother had to go to the hospital two weeks
before the expected time. I was wakened by her crying in the
night, and then I heard my father's footsteps as he went
downstairs to phone. I stood in the doorway of my room,
shivering and listening, wanting to go to my mother, but
afraid to go lest there be some sight there more terrifying than
I could bear.

"Hello, Paul?" my father said, and I knew he was talking
to Doctor Cates. "It's Beth. I'm only thinking of what
happened the last time, and another like that would be —
Yes, I think that would be the best thing. Okay, make it as
soon as you can."

He came back upstairs, looking bony and dishevelled in his
pyjamas, and running his fingers through his sand-coloured
hair. At the top of the stairs he came face to face with
Grandmother MacLeod, who was standing there in her quilted
black-satin dressing gown, her light figure held straight and
poised, as though she was unaware that her hair was bound
grotesquely like white-feathered wings in the snare of her
coarse night-time hairnet.

"What is it, Ewen?"

"It's all right, Mother. Beth's having . . . a little trouble.
I'm going to take her to the hospital. You go back to bed."

"I told you," Grandmother MacLeod said in her clear voice,
never loud, but distinct and ringing like the tap of a silver
spoon on a crystal goblet, "I did tell you, Ewen, did I not,
that you should have got a girl in to help her with the
housework? She should have rested more."

"I couldn't afford to get anyone in," my father said. "If you
thought she should've rested more, why didn't you ever . . .
Oh God, I'm out of my mind tonight. Just go back to bed,
Mother, please. I must get back to Beth."

When my father went down to open the front door for
Doctor Cates, my need overcame my fear and I slipped into
my parents' room. My mother's black hair, so neatly pinned

up during the day, was startlingly spread across the white pillowcase. I stared at her, not speaking, and then she smiled, and I rushed from the doorway and buried my head upon her.

"It's all right, Vanessa," she said. "Honey, the baby's just going to come a little early, that's all. You'll be all right. Grandmother MacLeod will be here."

"How can she get the meals?" I wailed, fixing on the first thing that came to mind. "She never cooks. She doesn't know how."

"Yes, she does," my mother said. "She can cook as well as anyone when she has to. She's just never had to very much, that's all. Don't worry, she'll keep everything in order, and then some."

My father and Doctor Cates came in, and I had to go, without saying anything I had wanted to say. I went back to my own room and lay with the shadows all around me, listening to the night murmurings that always went on in that house, sounds that never had a source — rafters and beams contracting in the dry air, perhaps, or mice in the walls, or a sparrow that had flown into the attic through the broken skylight there. After a while, although I would not have believed it possible, I slept.

The next morning, though summer vacation was not quite over, I did not feel like going out to play with any of the kids. I was very superstitious and felt that if I left the house, even for a few hours, some disaster would overtake my mother. I did not, of course, mention this to Grandmother MacLeod, for she did not believe in the existence of fear, or if she did, she never let on.

I spent the morning morbidly, seeking hidden places in the house. There were many of these — odd-shaped nooks under the stairs, and dusty tunnels and forgotten recesses in the heart of the house where the only things actually to be seen were drab oil paintings stacked upon the rafters and trunks full of out-moded clothing and old photograph albums. But the unseen presences in these secret places I knew to be those of every person, young or old, who had ever belonged to the house and had died, including Uncle Roderick who got killed on the Somme and the baby who would have been my sister if only she had come to life. Grandfather MacLeod, who had died a year after I was born, was present in the house in more tangible form. At the top of the main stairs hung a mammoth picture of a darkly uniformed man riding a horse whose prancing stance and dilated nostrils suggested the battle was not yet over, that it might continue until Judgment Day. The stern man was the Duke of Wellington, but at the time I believed him to be my Grandfather MacLeod, still keeping an eye on things.

We had moved in with Grandmother MacLeod when the depression got bad and she could no longer afford a housekeeper; yet the MacLeod house never seemed like home to me. Its dark-red brick was grown over at the front with Virginia creeper that turned crimson in the fall until you could hardly tell brick from leaves. It boasted a small tower in which Grandmother MacLeod kept a weed-like collection of anaemic ferns. The veranda was embellished with a profusion of wrought-iron scrolls, and the circular rose window upstairs contained many-coloured glass that permitted an outlooking eye to see the world as a place of absolute sapphire or emerald or, if one wished to look with a jaundiced eye, a hateful yellow. In Grandmother MacLeod's opinion, these features gave the house style. To me, they seemed fascinating, but rather as the paraphernalia of an alchemist's laboratory might be, things to be peered at curiously but with caution, just in case.

Inside, a multitude of doors led to rooms where my presence, if not actually forbidden, was not encouraged. One was Grandmother MacLeod's bedroom, with its stale and old-smelling reek of medicines and lavender sachets. Here resided her monogrammed dresser silver — brush and mirror, nail buffer and button hook and scissors — none of which must even be fingered by me now, for she meant to leave them to me in her will and intended to hand them over in their original flawless and unused condition. Here, too, were the silver-framed photographs of Uncle Roderick — as a child, as a boy, as a man in his army uniform. The massive walnut spool bed had obviously been designed for queens or giants, and my tiny grandmother used to lie within it all day when she had migraines, contriving somehow to look like a giant queen.

The day my mother went to the hospital, Grandmother MacLeod called me at lunch-time, and when I appeared, smudged with dust from the attic, she looked at me distastefully.

"For mercy's sake, Vanessa, what have you been doing with yourself? Get washed this minute. Not that way. Use the back stairs, young lady. Get along now. Oh, your father phoned."

I swung around. "What did he say? How is she? Is the baby born?"

"Curiosity killed the cat," Grandmother MacLeod said, frowning. "I cannot understand Beth and Ewen telling you all these things at your age. What sort of vulgar person you'll grow up to be, I dare not think. No, it's not born yet. Your mother's just the same. No change."

I looked at my grandmother, not wanting to appeal to her, but unable to stop myself. "Will she — will she be all right?"

Grandmother MacLeod straightened her already straight back. "If I said definitely yes, Vanessa, that would be a lie, and the MacLeods do not tell lies, as I have tried to impress upon you before. What happens is God's will. 'The Lord giveth, and the Lord taketh away.'"

Appalled, I turned away so she would not see my face. Surprisingly, I heard her sigh and felt her papery white and perfectly manicured hand upon my shoulder.

"When your Uncle Roderick got killed," she said, "I thought I would die. But I didn't die, Vanessa."

At lunch she chatted animatedly, and I realized she was trying to cheer me in the only way she knew. "When I

married your Grandfather MacLeod, he said to me, 'Eleanor,
don't think because we're going to the prairies that I expect
you to live roughly. You're used to a proper house, and you
shall have one.' He was as good as his word. Before we'd been
in Manawaka three years, he'd had this place built. He earned
a good deal of money in his time, your grandfather. He soon
had more patients than either of the other doctors. We ordered
our dinner service and all our silver from Birks in Toronto.
We had resident help in those days, of course, and never had
less than twelve guests for dinner parties. When I had a tea, it
would always be twenty or thirty. Never any less than half a
dozen different kinds of cake were ever served in this house.
Well, no one seems to bother much these days. Too lazy, I
suppose."

"Too broke," I suggested. "That's what Dad says."

"I can't bear slang," Grandmother MacLeod said. "If you
mean hard up, why don't you say so? It's mainly a question of
management, anyway. My accounts were always in good order,
and so was my house. No unexpected expenses that couldn't
be met, no fruit cellar running out of preserves before the
winter was over. Do you know what my father used to say to
me when I was a girl?"

"No," I said. "What?"

"'God loves order'," Grandmother MacLeod replied with
emphasis. "You remember that, Vanessa, 'God loves order'.
He wants each one of us to set our house in order. I've never
forgotten those words of my father's. I was a MacInnes before I
got married. The MacInnes is a very ancient clan, the lairds of
Morven and the constables of the Castle of Kinlochaline. Did
you finish that book I gave you?"

"Yes," I said. Then, feeling additional comment was called
for, I added, "It was a swell book, Grandmother."

This was somewhat short of the truth. I had been hoping
for her cairngorm brooch on my tenth birthday and had
received instead the plaid-bound volume entitled *The Clans and
Tartans of Scotland*. Most of it was too boring to read, but I
had looked up the motto of my own family and those of some

of my friends' families. *Be then a wall of brass. Learn to suffer. Consider the end. Go carefully.* I had not found any of these slogans reassuring. What with Mavis Duncan learning to suffer, and Laura Kennedy considering the end, and Patsy Drummond going carefully, and I spending my time in being a wall of brass, it did not seem to me that any of us were going to lead very interesting lives. I did not say this to Grandmother MacLeod.

"The MacInnes motto is *Pleasure arises from work*," I said.

"Yes," she agreed proudly. "And an excellent motto it is, too. One to bear in mind."

She rose from the table, rearranging on her bosom the looped ivory beads that held the pendant on which a full-blown ivory rose was stiffly carved.

"I hope Ewen will be pleased," she said.

"What at?"

"Didn't I tell you?" Grandmother MacLeod said. "I hired a girl this morning for the housework. She's to start tomorrow."

When my father got home that evening, Grandmother MacLeod told him her good news. He ran a hand distractedly across his forehead.

"I'm sorry, Mother, but you'll just have to unhire her. I can't possibly pay anyone."

"It seems odd," Grandmother MacLeod snapped, "that you can afford to eat chicken four times a week."

"Those chickens," my father said in an exasperated voice, "are how people are paying their bills. The same with the eggs and the milk. That scrawny turkey that arrived yesterday was for Logan MacCardney's appendix, if you must know. We probably eat better than any family in Manawaka, except Niall Cameron's. People can't entirely dispense with doctors or undertakers. That doesn't mean to say I've got any cash. Look, Mother, I don't know what's happening with Beth. Paul thinks he may have to do a Caesarean. Can't we leave all this? Just leave the house alone. Don't touch it. What does it matter?"

"I have never lived in a messy house, Ewen," Grandmother

MacLeod said, "and I don't intend to begin now."

"Oh, Lord," my father said. "Well, I'll phone Edna, I guess, and see if she can give us a hand, although God knows she's got enough, with the Connor house and her parents to look after."

"I don't fancy having Edna Connor in to help," Grandmother MacLeod said.

"Why not?" my father shouted. "She's Beth's sister, isn't she?"

"She speaks in such a slangy way," Grandmother MacLeod said. "I have never believed she was a good influence on Vanessa. And there is no need for you to raise your voice to me, Ewen, if you please."

I could barely control my rage. I thought my father would surely rise to Aunt Edna's defence. But he did not.

"It'll be all right," he soothed her. "She'd only be here for part of the day, Mother. You could stay in your room."

Aunt Edna strode in the next morning. The sight of her bobbed black hair and her grin made me feel better at once. She hauled out the carpet sweeper and the weighted polisher and got to work. I dusted while she polished and swept, and we got through the living room and front hall in next to no time.

"Where's her royal highness, kiddo?" she inquired.

"In her room," I said. "She's reading the catalogue from Robinson and Cleaver."

"Good glory, not again?" Aunt Edna cried. "The last time she ordered three linen tea towels and two dozen napkins. It came to fourteen dollars. Your mother was absolutely frantic. I guess I shouldn't be saying this."

"I knew anyway," I assured her. "She was at the lace-handkerchief section when I took up her coffee."

"Let's hope she stays there. Heaven forbid she should get onto the banqueting cloths. Well, at least she believes the Irish are good for two things — manual labor and

42

linen-making. She's never forgotten Father used to be a blacksmith, before he got the hardware store. Can you beat it? I wish it didn't bother Beth."

"Does it?" I asked and immediately realized this was a wrong move, for Aunt Edna was suddenly scrutinizing me.

"We're making you grow up before your time," she said. "Don't pay any attention to me, Nessa. I must've got up on the wrong side of the bed this morning."

But I was unwilling to leave the subject. "All the same," I said thoughtfully, "Grandmother MacLeod's family were the lairds of Morven and the constables of the Castle of Kinlochaline. I bet you didn't know that."

Aunt Edna snorted. "Castle, my foot. She was born in Ontario, just like your Grandfather Connor, and her father was a horse doctor. Come on, kiddo, we'd better shut up and get down to business here."

We worked in silence for a while.

"Aunt Edna," I said at last, "what about Mother? Why won't they let me go and see her?"

"Kids aren't allowed to visit maternity patients. It's tough for you, I know. Look, Nessa, don't worry. If it doesn't start tonight, they're going to do the operation. She's getting the best of care."

I stood there, holding the feather duster like a dead bird in my hands. I was not aware that I was going to speak until the words came out. "I'm scared," I said.

Aunt Edna put her arms around me, and her face looked all at once stricken and empty of defences.

"Oh, honey, I'm scared, too," she said.

It was this way that Grandmother MacLeod found us when she came stepping lightly down into the front hall with her order for two dozen lace-bordered handkerchiefs of pure Irish linen.

I could not sleep that night, and when I went downstairs, I found my father in the den. I sat down on the hassock beside his chair, and he told me about the operation my mother was to have the next morning. He kept saying it was not serious nowadays.

"But you're worried," I put in, as though seeking to explain why I was.

"I should at least have been able to keep from burdening you with it," he said in a distant voice, as though to himself. "If only the baby hadn't got twisted around — "

"Will it be born dead, like the little girl?"

"I don't know," my father said. "I hope not."

"She'd be disappointed, wouldn't she, if it was?" I said, wondering why I was not enough for her.

"Yes, she would," my father replied. "She won't be able to have any more, after this. It's partly on your account that she wants this one, Nessa. She doesn't want you to grow up without a brother or sister."

"As far as I'm concerned, she didn't need to bother."

My father laughed. "Well, let's talk about something else, and then maybe you'll be able to sleep. How did you and Grandmother make out today?"

"Oh, fine, I guess. What was Grandfather MacLeod like, Dad?"

"What did she tell you about him?"

"She said he made a lot of money in his time."

"Well, he wasn't any millionaire," my father said, "but I suppose he did quite well. That's not what I associate with him, though." He reached across to the bookshelf, took out a small leather-bound volume and opened it. On the pages were mysterious marks, like doodling, only much neater and more patterned.

"What is it?" I asked.

"Greek," my father explained. "This is a play called *Antigone*. See, here's the title in English. There's a whole stack of them on the shelves there. *Oedipus Rex. Electra. Medea.* They belonged to your Grandfather MacLeod. He used to read them often."

44

"Why?" I inquired, unable to understand why anyone would pore over those undecipherable signs.

"He was interested in them," my father said. "He must have been a lonely man, although it never struck me that way at the time. Sometimes a thing only hits you a long time afterward."

"Why would he be lonely?" I wanted to know.

"He was the only person in Manawaka who could read these plays in the original Greek," my father said. "I don't suppose many people, if anyone, had even read them in English translation. Maybe he once wanted to be a classical scholar — I don't know. But his father was a doctor, so that's what he was. Maybe he would have liked to talk to somebody about these plays. They must have meant a lot to him."

It seemed to me that my father was talking oddly. There was a sadness in his voice that I had never heard before, and I longed to say something that would make him feel better, but I could not, because I did not know what was the matter.

"Can you read this kind of writing?" I asked hesitantly.

My father shook his head. "Nope. I was never very intellectual, I guess. Your Uncle Roderick was always brighter than I, in school, but even he wasn't interested in learning Greek. Perhaps he would've been later, if he'd lived. As a kid, all I ever wanted to do was go into the merchant marine."

"Why didn't you?"

"Oh, well," my father said, "a kid who'd never seen the sea wouldn't have made much of a sailor. I might have turned out to be the seasick type."

I had lost interest, now that he was once more speaking like himself.

"Grandmother MacLeod was pretty cross today about the girl," I said.

"I know," my father said. "Well, we must be as nice as we can to her, Nessa, and after a while she'll be all right."

Suddenly I did not care what I said.

"Why can't she be nice to *us* for a change?" I burst out.

"We're always the ones who have to be nice to her."

My father put his hand down and tilted my head until I was forced to look at him. "Vanessa," he said, "she's had troubles in her life which you really don't know much about. That's why she sometimes gets migraines and has to go to bed. It's not easy for her these days. The house is still the same, so she thinks other things should be, too. It hurts her when she finds they aren't."

"I don't see — " I began.

"Listen," my father said, "you know we were talking just now about what people are interested in, like Grandfather MacLeod being interested in Greek plays? Well, your grandmother was interested in being a lady, Nessa, and for a long time it seemed to her that she was one."

I thought of the Castle of Kinlochaline and of horse doctors in Ontario.

"I didn't know — " I stammered.

"That's usually the trouble with most of us," my father said. "Now you go on up to bed. I'll phone tomorrow from the hospital as soon as the operation's over."

I did sleep at last, and in my dreams I could hear the caught sparrow fluttering in the attic and the sound of my mother crying and the voices of dead children.

My father did not phone until afternoon. Although Grandmother MacLeod said I was being silly, for you could hear the phone ringing all over the house, I refused to move out of the den. I had never before examined my father's books, but now, at a loss for something to do, I took them out one by one and read snatches here and there. After several hours, it dawned on me that most of the books were of the same kind. I looked again at the titles.

Seven League Boots. Travels in Arabia Deserta. The Seven Pillars of Wisdom. Travels in Tartary, Thibet and China. Count Luckner, the Sea Devil. And a hundred more. On a shelf by themselves were copies of the *National Geographic Magazine.* I had looked at these often enough, but never with the puzzling compulsion

46

which I felt now, as though I was on the verge of some discovery, something which I had to find out and yet did not want to know. I riffled through the picture-filled pages. Hibiscus and wild orchids grew in soft-petaled profusion. The Himalayas stood lofty as gods, with the morning sun on their peaks of snow. Leopards snarled from the depth of a thousand jungles. Schooners buffeted their white sails like the wings of giant angels against the sea winds.

"What on earth are you doing?" Grandmother MacLeod inquired waspishly, from the doorway. "You've got everything scattered all over the place. Pick it all up this minute, Vanessa, do you hear?" So I picked up the books and magazines and put them neatly away.

When the telephone finally rang, I was afraid to answer it. At last I did. My father sounded far away, and the relief in his voice made it unsteady.

"It's okay, honey. Everything's fine. The boy was born alive and kicking after all. Your mother's pretty weak, but she's going to be all right."

I could hardly believe it. I did not want to talk to anyone. I wanted to be by myself, to assimilate the presence of my brother, toward whom, without even having seen him, I felt such tenderness and such resentment.

That evening, Grandmother MacLeod approached my father, who at first did not take her seriously when she asked what they planned to call the child.

"Oh, I don't know. Hank, maybe, or Joe. Fauntleroy, perhaps."

She ignored his levity. "Ewen, I wish you would call him Roderick."

His face changed. "I'd rather not."

"I think you should," Grandmother MacLeod insisted, in a voice as pointed and precise as her silver nail scissors.

"Don't you think Beth ought to decide?" my father asked.

"Beth will agree if you do."

My father did not bother to deny something that even I

knew to be true. He did not say anything. Then Grandmother MacLeod's voice, astonishingly, faltered a little. "It would mean a great deal to me," she said.

I remembered what she had told me — *When your Uncle Roderick got killed, I thought I would die. But I didn't die.* All at once her feeling for that unknown dead man became a reality for me. And yet I held it against her, as well, for I could see that she was going to win now.

"All right," my father said. "We'll call him Roderick."

Then, alarmingly, he threw back his head and laughed. "Roderick Dhu!" he cried. "That's what you'll call him, isn't it? Black Roderick. Like before. Don't you remember? As though he was a character out of Sir Walter Scott, instead of an ordinary kid who — "

He broke off and looked at her with a kind of desolation in his face.

"God, I'm sorry, Mother," he said. "I had no right to say that."

Grandmother MacLeod did not flinch, or tremble, or indicate that she felt anything at all. "I accept your apology, Ewen," she said.

My mother had to stay in bed for several weeks after she arrived home. The baby's crib was kept in my parents' room, and I could go in and look at the small creature who lay there with his tightly closed fists and his feathery black hair. Aunt Edna came in to help each morning, and when she had finished the housework, she would have coffee with my mother. They kept the door closed, but this did not prevent me from eavesdropping, for there was an air register in the floor of the spare room that was linked somehow with the register in my parents' room. If you put your ear to the iron grille, it was almost like a radio.

"Did you mind very much, Beth?" Aunt Edna was saying.

"Oh, it's not the name I mind," my mother replied. "It's just that Ewen felt he had to. You knew that Rod only had the sight of one eye, didn't you?"

48

"Sure, I knew. So what?"

"There was only a year and a half between Ewen and Rod," my mother said, "so they often went around together when they were youngsters. It was Ewen's air rifle that did it."

"Oh, Lord," Aunt Edna said. "I suppose she always blamed him?"

"No, I don't think it was so much that, really. It was how he felt himself. I think he even used to wonder sometimes if — but people shouldn't let themselves think like that, or they'd go crazy. Accidents do happen, after all. When the war came, Ewen joined up first. Rod should never have been in the army at all, but he couldn't wait to get in. He must have lied about his eyesight. It wasn't so very noticeable unless you looked at him closely, and I don't suppose the medicals were very thorough in those days. He got in as a gunner, and Ewen applied to have him in the same company. He thought he might be able to watch out for him, I guess, Rod being at a disadvantage. They were both only kids. Ewen was nineteen and Rod was eighteen when they went to France. And then the Somme. I don't know, Edna, I think Ewen felt that if Rod had had proper sight, or if he hadn't been in the same outfit and had been sent somewhere else — you know how people always think these things afterward, not that it's ever a bit of use. Ewen wasn't there when Rod got hit. They'd lost each other somehow, and Ewen was looking for him, not bothering about anything else, you know, just frantically looking. Then he stumbled across him quite by chance. Rod was still alive, but — "

"Stop it, Beth," Aunt Edna said. "You're only upsetting yourself."

"Ewen never spoke of it to me," my mother went on, "until his mother showed me the letter he'd written to her at the time. It was a peculiar letter, almost formal, saying how gallantly Rod had died, and all that. I guess I shouldn't have, but I told him she'd shown it to me. He was very angry that she had. And then, as though for some reason he was terribly ashamed, he said, 'I had to write something to her, but men don't really die like that, Beth. It wasn't that way at all.' It was only after the war that he decided to study medicine and go into practice with his father."

"Had Rod meant to?" Aunt Edna asked.

"I don't know," my mother said. "I never felt I should ask Ewen that."

Aunt Edna was gathering up the coffee things, for I could hear the clash of cups and saucers being stacked on the tray. "You know what I heard her say to Vanessa once, Beth? *'The MacLeods never tell lies.'* Those were her exact words. Even then, I didn't know whether to laugh or cry."

"Please Edna." My mother sounded worn out now. "Don't."

"Oh, glory," Aunt Edna said, "I've got all the delicacy of a two-ton truck. I didn't mean Ewen, for heaven's sake. That wasn't what I meant at all. Here, let me plump up your pillows for you."

Then the baby began to cry, so I could not hear anything more of interest. I took my bike and went out beyond Manawaka, riding aimlessly along the gravel highway. It was late summer, and the wheat had changed colour, but instead of being high and bronzed in the fields, it was stunted and desiccated, for there had been no rain again this year. Yet on the bluff where I stopped and crawled under the barbed-wire fence and lay stretched out on the grass, the plentiful poplar leaves were turning to a luminous yellow and shone like church windows in the sun. I put my head down very close to the earth and looked at what was going on there. Grasshoppers with enormous eyes ticked and twitched around me, as though the dry air was perfect for their purposes. A ladybug laboured mightily to climb a blade of grass, fell off and started all over again, seeming to be unaware that she possessed wings and could have flown up.

I thought of the accidents that might easily happen to a person — or, of course, might not happen, might happen to somebody else. I thought of the dead baby, my sister, who might as easily have been I. Would she, then, have been lying here in my place, the sharp grass making its small toothmarks on her brown arms, the sun warming her to the heart? I thought of the leather-bound volumes of Greek, and of the six different kinds of iced cakes that used to be offered always in the MacLeod house, and of the pictures of leopards and green seas. I thought of my brother, who had been born alive after all, and now had been given his life's name.

I could not really comprehend these things, but I sensed their strangeness, their disarray. I felt that whatever God might love in this world, it was certainly not order.

LINES IN CONTENTMENT
Gail Fox

(for Milton)

My son, whose small age
barely confirms my motherhood,
sings into my sleep
with hungry insistence
and catches me always
on the verge of forgetting
who I now am and must be:
loving, honest, possessed of my senses.
I pick him up and
he grows in my hands,
grows into each successive morning,
singing me into a semblance of identity.
He grows, and in his excessive joy,
takes me along.

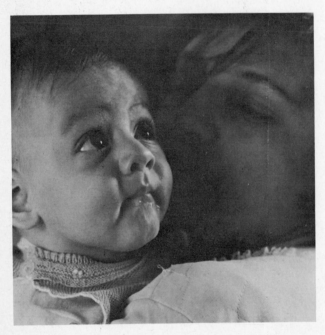

DANGEROUS SEASON
Gail Fox

I think you meant to rake
yesterday, today I did it
and found green shoots
pushing up, accusingly.
I gripped the rake harder
and stood where you
would have stood, uneasy
with the raw look of things,
unable to leave the place
where grass blades began
to travel to the trees,
their shadows cutting
deeply on my feet.

Did you mean to rake
yesterday? Sometimes I don't
know what you mean and
I stand in places where
you would stand and
find that nothing is safe,
spring arriving and lighting
its pale, green fuse . . .

I'M SORRY MRS. STRAUSS
Mary Soderstrom

Mrs. Strauss was Polish. The Strausses lived across the street in the two-bedroom house with the only basement in the neighbourhood. I never liked the house, I didn't like her, and I didn't want her at my wedding.

Mr. Strauss was German and the produce manager at the big chain grocery up by the high school. He never said much but Mrs. Strauss made up for that. She said: that Adlai Stevenson would never be president because the women of America would never elect a divorced man; that nice colored people didn't want to mix any more than white folks did; that she didn't worry about her older daughter who was pretty but slow because "I never said anything until I was 18 either"; and that it didn't matter whether or not she was invited to our wedding because she'd just slip in the back door of the church and watch, "unless you Protestants have some rule about that."

Of course she wasn't the only Pole we knew — the husband of one of the girls in Dad's office was Polish, from some industrial town in the East. But in San Diego at that time the only people who stood out as a group were Mexicans and Portuguese. "He's not like the rest of them," my friend Mellissa had said about the boy who'd asked her to the Starlight Opera. "He's different. Otherwise I'd never look at a Portaghee."

But Poland? Well, it had been partitioned four times by Germany and Russia. It was in the north where it was cold and wet. It made hams which certain right-wing groups were boycotting. But aside from that: zero. Who knew and who cared? Then the dreams came with the winter of the year when forces beyond me pushed Barney north to Montreal and to a country I could not understand.

The first dream is the castle on a frozen marsh with big black birds — crows — circling around. The land is very flat but the horizon seems waist high, so the brooding enormity of the cold, still plain presses down on you. It is Poland, I know. The sky fits tightly over the land; it is not the big high sky of the plains we know where the height is a challenge to soar.

I tell Barney about it in the morning, pressed close to him to escape the cold wind blowing through the crack under the window.

"Crows are supposed to be a sign of spring around here," he says cheerfully.

But a week later I dream it again, followed quickly by another dream. In the second a wolf is chasing me across the frozen swamp. I look down and see the flowers of the fall quick-frozen under foot. There are asters and daisies and green grass encased in the ice. I think of hills that are green in December, where the sun always shines, and things grow all year long, and I start to cry. As the tears fall to the ice, they turn into a mirror. Suddenly it is like running through space, with the sun above and below, and all around blue and brilliant, searing light. But I glance behind to see that the wolf is no longer a wolf, but part wolf, part man, part skeleton, with bones sticking through the wolf's mangy coat, and the smell of putrefaction rises in the air. Then I realize that the landscape of ice and light is changeless and I am not moving no matter how fast I run.

Barney is shaking me, asking me what is the matter. My eyes feel swollen as if I'd been crying all night, and my throat hurts. The pillow is wet with tears.

"Nothing," I tell him. "Just a dream like the other one. Nothing to be worried about." I do not want the terror spoiled by his comfortable concern or rational explanations. But why Poland? I am frightened. That day I am afraid to open the door, to go downstairs, to cook on the hot plate.

"For Christ's sake," Barney explodes. "It's electric, not gas, damn it. It won't blow up."

And then I feel more sorry for him than for me. We are supposed to be doing this together. He has seen so many worse things.

Yesterday I read a story in the paper about animals. The paper was lining the drawer in the night-stand and, since the sun was shining, I decided to clean things up. But I read the paper instead. I read it over and over, although it was two years old. It was about animals which are dying out; the leopard, the elephants, certain birds, jaguars, and cheetahs. But it added that tigers seemed to be on the increase in Indo-China, "as wolves increased in Poland during the Second World War. Both will feed on human corpses."

Poland.

It cannot be colder or more dismal than this country where the shining sun brings its special kind of misery.

"We get some of our finest weather in the winter," the lady in the fur hat told me. "It may be 10 below but the air is so crystal clear and the sun is blinding."

Like the dream, I think; the only thing missing in it was the fire on your skin from the cold. I want to run barefoot out of doors. I want to smell plants. But Poland; why do I feel myself falling toward it?

Barney made me go out with him today, walk the two blocks down the slippery street to the campus. It is almost the shortest day of the year and by four o'clock the sun was already setting behind the hill they call a mountain.

"Look up," he said when I said something about the rotten weather. I did without thinking, quickly, faster than I had moved in a week. The sky was the thin green of sea water, turning pale yellow and then pink at the edge tucked in behind the hill. How dare he make me see that! I did not want to go on but when I saw the gray faces of the people in the street light I was more afraid of being left by myself.

The feast of the winter solstice; now I see why they clung so stubbornly to it, those Northern Christians. It is as if the world were slowly ending, each night taking more and more of the light until it seems there's hardly any left.

We went to the Christmas party last night. It was cold and

snowing, but Barney wanted to go, I could see that. He's been happy this week. They like what he is doing here; one of them asked if he would like to stay. That's why we came of course; to find a place to stay, away from the memories. Away from that war, over but unforgotten.

The party was important, he said — if the others like him, too, hear good things about him, there might be something permanent next year; peace and library privileges. He always did like libraries. He would hide there when I first knew him. And peace was always what he said he wanted. I misunderstood what he meant; the fault was mine, perhaps.

So I smiled and washed my hair, ironed him a shirt from the stack that had sat in the pile since the second week we were here and I first felt the cold in the air, and the fear. He watched. "Put that stuff on your eyes," he said. "And why don't you wear those dangly earrings? You always look so pretty in them." Shy voice; sometimes I forget he has it. Like his mother, slow and gentle and lean on words. Sometimes I forget that I love that too.

We took a taxi, not the bus. The place was on the 14th floor, high up on the mountain. I could see all the lights of the downtown buildings and the bridges across the river and houses on the other side. There was a full moon that outlined the lonely hills that rise out of the plain. For a while I stood looking out the window, hearing the voices behind me like water breaking on cliffs. I could feel myself wanting to sail down and down into the yellow-lighted canyons just as I always want to dive to the bottom where the breaking waves cannot touch me.

"I'd like you to meet my wife," Barney said, dragging over the man nearest him. He was Janos Something. He kissed my hand.

"Enchanté," he said.

"How do you do?" I said, ill at ease.

He was shorter than I, with white hair, neat around the neck but falling forward to his eyebrows. His eyes were strong and there was something stiff about him, like machinery or memories of being caned for bad manners.

A Pole? I wondered. Then, suddenly bold, I asked.

"I was born in Warsaw, but I left in 1938." He bowed slightly. "I have been in this country since 1952. I am a citizen."

"Oh," I said.

We stood stiffly for a moment, each wondering what to say.

Then: "Do you like Montreal?" I asked.

He took a sip of his drink and looked out the windows at the white and navy and gold night. "I find it very pleasant." He hesitated, as if he wondered if I'd understood, if I were interested. "But it is not Warsaw." And he made a shadow of a bow again.

"You have been back then?"

He smiled as if that were a silly question. "Four times since the war. Some of my family survived, you see."

"Oh," I said. I wanted to ask, have you heard about the wolves and the tigers?

"I would like to go back again," he said. "There is something in the air there, something lively in the way the people walk and the women dress. Do you know London?"

I made a noise.

"The last time I was in Europe I went to Warsaw direct from London, and I was struck by the contrast. London seemed so cheerless. Mind you, I am very fond of London, too. That is where I went after I left Poland."

And why did you leave? I wanted to ask. Because you saw the writing on the wall? Because you knew the Poles? And yet you still love Warsaw?

It is my turn now, and I can think of nothing to say aside from a list of questions no one would want to answer. I glance over his shoulder and see the dark trees of the mountain through the corner window. How cold it is. How bad things must have been for him and all the others to want to come here, a few acres of snow, a country called winter.

"Is it very cold there, in Poland?" I ask.

He looks at me, surprised again. For a second he is tempted

to answer politely and then to escape. But I can see he wonders about my question, perhaps smells my fear.

"Cold? Yes, it can be cold. Why do you ask?"

"And the people? In the country what do they do all winter? Is there enough food? Are they warm?"

He chuckles. "What have you been reading? These are modern times. Everyone has trucks and railroad trains and electricity."

"Oh," I say. Maybe, I think.

He begins to talk about the smallness of the world, how the Japanese are importing denim to make blue jeans, and I listen soberly. What I want to know is: what happens to all the cruelty when we are civilized? What about Warsaw? What about the wolves?

Mrs. Strauss, I remember, gave us three presents. Two were shower gifts — a waste basket and a cookie jar — and I wrote her as I wrote all my mother's friends, thanking her profusely. Then, the day before the wedding she brought over the wedding present. I could see her coming across the street, and I wanted to hide but my mother wouldn't let me.

"Thank you, thank you," I said, as I fumbled with the package. And I was even more embarrassed when I saw it was a coffee pot, something I'd been wanting.

"But, Mom, it's my wedding not yours. I don't approve of her. She's ignorant and talkative and a bigot and she wouldn't fit in," I said after she had left. My mother, my kind mother, only looked at me sadly, until I had to go and find the last of the invitations and take it across the street. There was no answer when I rang the bell, and I didn't ring it more than once. I put the envelope in the mail box and ran back across the road, quickly, not letting the hot asphalt burn my bare feet.

I can't remember if she came to the wedding or not. I wouldn't have if I'd been her. Still, it's a lovely evening. Even in this god-forsaken climate one can almost forget about the wolves.

THE GARDENERS

Jay Macpherson

My next neighbour
Worked herself to bone
Raising prize bokays
In a yard mostly stone.
I'd be rocking
On the back stoop,
And she'd say my yard
Looked like a chicken coop.

Bet you she's raging
Over in her plot:
Nary a stalk but
Couchgrass she's got.
Can't grow nothing better
On the likes of she,
But I lie pushing daisies
Fat and white as me.

SPRINGTIME
Claire Martin

(Translated by Philip Stratford)

The neighbours laughed when Miss Amelia went by. The women would shrug their shoulders, which set their bountiful breasts bouncing under their flowered housecoats. The children, repeating what they had heard their parents say, would shout after her, "Crazy old maid! Crazy old maid!"

Miss Amelia wouldn't even deign to lift an eyelid. Stiffly, in her black dress, she would pass on by.

Poor Amelia. It's true she was still a maid, but she wasn't old. Thirty-five, thirty-eight maybe. In the prime of life. And not ugly either. But her face was always ravaged by rage.

From the back she was enticing enough to be followed frequently. By men who were strangers to the neighbourhood, it should be noted. Anger, her daily bread, kept her as thin as a garter snake, gave a spring to her step, and an extraordinary toss to her head. Compared to the old housefraus on the block, she made you think of an unbroken mare in a field of fat cows.

The follower, being attracted to nervous women, would trot along behind. Drawing abreast, he would stop dumbfounded, then hurry right on by. There wasn't a single one who ever thought of anything but escape, followed by the laughter of the natives.

She had a look like a bull whip, did Miss Amelia. You really had to be a stranger not to know its devastating effects.

There was only one person, the lady who lived on the third floor left, who tried to be kind to her. It wasn't easy, yet she didn't give up trying. She was the persevering sort, a woman who followed her notions right through to the end.

Since she was going through her third husband, Miss Amelia's case seemed triply pathetic to her. "The poor thing," she would sigh. "Just put yourself in her shoes. Have you seen those red hot coals in her eyes? She's burning up, she is! It's all very well to say, better marry than burn. But Saint Paul doesn't say what to do when you're only a woman and no husband comes forward."

With that she would pull a little pout for the misogynist saint and then dissolve in pretty smiles and confusion. In her case, husbands flocked forward like indigents to a soup kitchen.

It was mainly her brother Charles, lately come to the neighbourhood, whom the wife from the third floor left chose as confidant for her compassion. Charles was fortyish, a shoemaker, and a good-looking man. And like his sister he had a heart that was tender and understanding.

The day he saw the old maid come into his shop with her offended face, he couldn't resist the sudden urge to be a little bit nice to her, just to see. A compliment is quickly made, doesn't cost anything, and can't lead very far. As he was a shoemaker, he looked at her foot, quickly saw that it was slender and nicely arched, and told her as much.

Now it so happened that Miss Amelia had always been quite proud of her feet. Perhaps she had always been waiting for someone to say something nice about them. Perhaps that was all she held against the human race, their ignorance of the fact that her feet existed. Her expression softened. She inclined her head gently and gave a little laugh as fresh as a schoolgirl's upon leaving the convent at the end of term.

Down she sat, took off her shoe, and put her foot up on the low stool. Charles felt impelled to rush forward, he knew he should have, but he stood there like a simpleton. The sparkle of her teeth, the curve of her foot, the caress of her laugh, had gone straight to his heart, and he was filled with a kind of fearful joy.

When the worst of his emotion had passed, he got out his finest shoes, shoes that were supple and soft as a girl's cheek. He could see how his trembling hands gave him away, but he didn't care. If a man doesn't speak, you can't slap him for trembling, can you? And apart from a slap he was ready for anything.

62

Courage! The moment had come. He seized her foot with just the right degree of warmth and slipped it into the shoe. "It fits like a glove! And you notice I didn't even ask your size." It was true. This happy stroke seemed to lend the whole affair a flavour of predestination that was troublesome indeed.

He stayed there holding the narrow foot closely in his hand. She felt the burn through the leather. Silently she savoured this unknown happiness, thinking all the while that the other foot was cold too. He let her have the shoes at cost. For him she was already almost the boss. At cost price. And he blushed when he took the money.

Miss Amelia's romance left the neighbourhood stunned and bewildered. The news dominated the conversations of the local gossips. Doors and windows filled with heads as she passed by.

That the old maid was loved and in love was already grist to their mill, but even more astounding was her new physical appearance. Each day that went by put a little more velvet in her look, a little more satin to her skin, and a sort of abandon in the roll of her hips. Now her ankles betrayed her and she would stumble when she walked out under Charles' admiring gaze. Her knees buckled under the miracle.

The grocer's wife, who had been chosen by her husband because she was solidly built and could stay on her feet behind the counter twelve hours at a stretch without grumbling, and who had accepted because the grocery business is the most serious of all commercial enterprises, followed this metamorphosis with an astonished eye and sighed all day long.

Charles' sister came close to believing that there must be a strain of sorcery in the family. She talked to her third husband at great length about it. So much so that the poor man began to get shivers down his spine whenever she looked at him, as she often did now with a mildly haggard expression as if seeing through him. He couldn't help feeling that the spell hadn't been exhausted yet and that it was a fourth chance at happiness his wife was watching as it advanced through the promise-laden fog of the future.

When Amelia and Charles announced their marriage, the neighbourhood breathed a sigh of relief. At last things were going to return to normal. Everyone had managed to survive the courtship, but it would be nice to get back to preoccupations a little less torrid. By the wedding day, interest was already on the wane. The lovers were turning out just like everyone else.

A month hadn't passed before a little of the old Miss Amelia — just a trifle — began to show through. At first just a slight tensing of the nostrils. A few weeks later and it had spread to her mouth. After six months she had got back the two furrows between her eyebrows. Nobody noticed because nobody was particularly interested any more. From time to time they would size up the state of her belly, but when that showed no signs of change they thought about something else.

It wasn't till months later that two old cronies, whiling away their time pinching lettuce heads, were struck by a sense of *déjà vu* when Miss Amelia walked by. She had completely recovered her prancing gait, her furious face, and her whiplash look.

The two old women burst out laughing and began slapping their thighs. After all, nobody expected that dreamy mood to last a lifetime, did they?

Poor Amelia, would she ever remember anything about that spring, that gentle madness, that brief blossoming?

JEWELLERY
Gwendolyn MacEwen

I wear it more to be its captive
than to captivate; I want
to be the prisoner of gold,
to hear my voice break through
the chain which holds my song
in check, or watch the tendons
flicker under
the band about my wrist
which makes my gestures
conscious and restrained;
the circular earrings
familiar as my name
have tamed my mind
as the single ring
has tamed my hand.

You have made a glittering prison
of all my jewellery,
you knew I never wanted
to be free.

REAL WOMEN IN FICTION, WHERE ARE YOU?
Doris Anderson

"Have you any notion how many books are written about women in the course of one year? Have you any notion how many are written by men? Are you aware that you are, perhaps, the most discussed animal in the universe?" Virginia Woolf, in 1929, in *A Room of One's Own*, protested that women needed privacy and time to think about and interpret themselves.

For the past two years books about women by women have been flicking off the presses like newly minted razor blades. Some are scholarly and heavily researched. Others are clip-and-paste assembly jobs of feminist authors, and still others are treatises bristling with suppressed rage and frustration.

For far too long women have been interpreted through the eyes of men — as Virginia Woolf complained. (If Catherine in *A Farewell to Arms* behaved strangely to you, small wonder. She had been fashioned by Hemingway as a romantic ornament in a completely male novel.)

Personally, I long for the day when the consciousness-raising exercises in the analytical and scholarly books on women are translated into fiction. In all of fiction, writers who interpreted women with insight are rare — Jane Austen, George Eliot, Arnold Bennett, Virginia Woolf, Proust, Joyce, Tolstoi, Mary McCarthy are a few.

North American writers have been particularly obtuse in writing about women. In *Life and Death in the American Novel*, Leslie Fiedler points out that male North American writers either exalted women as near-saints, or more often, depicted them as bitch-goddesses to be feared and ultimately killed. The saints, who usually died young, tended to be prissy and characterless. They even bored their own creators so much that many male writers preferred instead to write about struggling against nature, or conquering frontiers — or whales. Anything seemed more interesting than women. Quite often the male heroes of North American novels, according to Fiedler, never grew up. Tom Sawyer and Huckleberry Finn still appear in modern dress in Hemingway, Mailer, Salinger, and Kerouac. They are at ease only in a womanless world. Love and marriage are the end of boyhood and to be avoided.

Often a romantic reunion with the faithful, saintly heroine was used as a device to end the chronicle in the last chapter, after the hero had conquered fire, flood, savages, etc., etc. Or, more often, the heroine died.

Detectives, claims Fiedler, are really cowboys on city streets. They are antifemale and, like Mike Hammer, rape and kill women again and again.

As for North American women writers, their fiction is often too self-absorbed and genteel. The oversensitive heroines suffer and suffer, not only from the rawness of North American life but from their own psychological flagellations.

There are two other kinds of heroine, particularly in British novels. One is the victim of numerous hair-raising escapes in Gothic romances. The other is the perky character in conventional romance. (Nice girl goes on a trip, meets slightly sinister stranger who later turns out not only to be rich and titled but madly in love with her.)

Now that women are writing about themselves in psychological, sociological, and historical terms it's time for some bonuses in the way of living, breathing fictional heroines. We're far more complex than the limited roles assigned to us by super jocks like Hemingway and Norman Mailer. We're far more vital and capable of dealing with the world than the wispy, sensitive heroines of much of the fiction that has been written by females. Isn't it possible to write about mature, intelligent, passionate women with grace, vigor, and humor?

Until that happy day, I'll be watching eagerly.

THE LEAN GIRL
Anne Hébert

(Translated by F. R. Scott)

I am a lean girl
And I have beautiful bones.

I tend them with great care
And feel strange pity for them.

I continually polish them
As though they were old metal.

Now jewels and flowers
Are out of season.

One day I shall clasp my lover
And make of him a silver shrine.

I shall hang myself
In the place of his absent heart.

O well-filled space,
What is this cold guest suddenly in you?

You walk,
You move;
Each one of your gestures
Adorns with fear the enclosed death.

I receive your trembling
As a gift.

And sometimes
Fastened in your breast,
I half open
My liquid eyes

As strange and childish dreams
Swirl
Like green water.

THE FOUND BOAT
Alice Munro

At the end of Bell Street, McKay Street, Mayo Street, there
was the Flood. It was the Wawanash River, which every
spring overflowed its banks. Some springs, say one in every
five, it covered the roads on that side of town and washed over
the fields, creating a shallow choppy lake. Light reflected off
the water made everything bright and cold, as it is in a
lakeside town, and woke or revived in people certain vague
hopes of disaster. Mostly during the late afternoon and early
evening, there were people straggling out to look at it, and
discuss whether it was still rising, and whether this time it
might invade the town. In general, those under fifteen and
over sixty-five were most certain that it would.

Eva and Carol rode out on their bicycles. They left the road
— it was the end of Mayo Street, past any houses — and rode
right into a field, over a wire fence entirely flattened by the
weight of the winter's snow. They coasted a little way before
the long grass stopped them, then left their bicycles lying
down and went to the water.

"We have to find a log and ride on it," Eva said.

"Jesus, we'll freeze our legs off."

"Jesus, we'll freeze our legs off!" said one of the boys who
were there too at the water's edge. He spoke in a sour whine,
the way boys imitated girls although it was nothing like the
way girls talked. These boys — there were three of them —
were all in the same class as Eva and Carol at school and were
known to them by name (their names being Frank, Bud, and
Clayton), but Eva and Carol, who had seen and recognized
them from the road, had not spoken to them or looked at
them or, even yet, given any sign of knowing they were there.
The boys seemed to be trying to make a raft, from lumber
they had salvaged from the water.

Eva and Carol took off their shoes and socks and waded in.
The water was so cold it sent pain up their legs, like blue
electric sparks shooting through their veins, but they went on,
pulling their skirts high, tight behind and bunched so they
could hold them in front.

"Look at the fat-assed ducks in wading."

Eva and Carol, of course, gave no sign of hearing this. They laid hold of a log and climbed on, taking a couple of boards floating in the water for paddles. There were always things floating around in the Flood — branches, fence-rails, logs, road signs, old lumber; sometimes boilers, washtubs, pots and pans, or even a car seat or stuffed chair, as if somewhere the Flood had got into a dump.

They paddled away from shore, heading out into the cold lake. The water was perfectly clear, they could see the brown grass swimming along the bottom. Suppose it was the sea, thought Eva. She thought of drowned cities and countries. Atlantis. Suppose they were riding in a Viking boat — Viking boats on the Atlantic were more frail and narrow than this log on the Flood — and they had miles of clear sea beneath them, then a spired city, intact as a jewel irretrievable on the ocean floor.

"This is a Viking boat," she said. "I am the carving on the front." She stuck her chest out and stretched her neck, trying to make a curve, and she made a face, putting out her tongue. Then she turned and for the first time took notice of the boys.

"Hey, you sucks!" she yelled at them. "You'd be scared to come out here, this water is ten feet deep!"

"Liar," they answered without interest, and she was.

They steered the log around a row of trees, avoiding floating barbed wire, and got into a little bay created by a natural hollow of the land. Where the bay was now, there would be a pond full of frogs later in the spring, and by the middle of summer there would be no water visible at all, just a low tangle of reeds and bushes, green, to show that mud was still wet around their roots. Larger bushes, willows, grew around the steep bank of this pond and were still partly out of the water. Eva and Carol let the log ride in. They saw a place where something was caught.

It was a boat, or part of one. An old rowboat with most of one side ripped out, the board that had been the seat just dangling. It was pushed up among the branches, lying on what would have been its side, if it had a side, the prow caught high.

Their idea came to them without consultation, at the same time:

"You guys! Hey, you guys!"

"We found you a boat!"

"Stop building your stupid raft and come and look at the boat!"

What surprised them in the first place was that the boys really did come, scrambling overland, half running, half sliding down the bank, wanting to see.

"Hey, where?"

"Where is it, I don't see no boat."

What surprised them in the second place was that when the boys did actually see what boat was meant, this old flood-smashed wreck held up in the branches, they did not understand that they had been fooled, that a joke had been played on them. They did not show a moment's disappointment, but seemed as pleased at the discovery as if the boat had been whole and new. They were already barefoot, because they had been wading in the water to get lumber, and they waded in here without a stop, surrounding the boat and appraising it and paying no attention even of an insulting kind to Eva and Carol who bobbed up and down on their log. Eva and Carol had to call to them.

"How do you think you're going to get it off?"

"It won't float anyway."

"What makes you think it will float?"

"It'll sink. Glub-blub-blub, you'll all be drownded."

The boys did not answer, because they were too busy walking around the boat, pulling at it in a testing way to see how it could be got off with the least possible damage. Frank, who was the most literate, talkative, and inept of the three, began referring to the boat as *she*, an affectation which Eva and Carol acknowledged with fish-mouths of contempt.

"She's caught two places. You got to be careful not to tear a hole in her bottom. She's heavier than you'd think."

It was Clayton who climbed up and freed the boat, and Bud, a tall fat boy, who got the weight of it on his back to turn it into the water so that they could half float, half carry it to shore. All this took some time. Eva and Carol abandoned their log and waded out of the water. They walked overland to get their shoes and socks and bicycles. They did not need to come back this way but they came. They stood at the top of the hill, leaning on their bicycles. They did not go on home, but they did not sit down and frankly watch, either. They stood more or less facing each other, but glancing down at the water and at the boys struggling with the boat, as if they had just halted for a moment out of curiosity, and staying longer than they intended, to see what came of this unpromising project.

About nine o'clock, or when it was nearly dark — dark to people inside the houses, but not quite dark outside — they all returned to town, going along Mayo Street in a sort of procession. Frank and Bud and Clayton came carrying the boat, upside-down, and Eva and Carol walked behind, wheeling their bicycles. The boys' heads were almost hidden in the darkness of the overturned boat, with its smell of soaked wood, cold swampy water. The girls could look ahead and see the street lights in their tin reflectors, a necklace of lights climbing Mayo Street, reaching all the way up to the standpipe. They turned onto Burns Street heading for Clayton's house, the nearest house belonging to any of them. This was not the way home for Eva or for Carol either, but they followed along. The boys were perhaps too busy carrying the boat to tell them to go away. Some younger children were still out playing, playing hopscotch on the sidewalk though they could hardly see. At this time of year the bare sidewalk was still such a novelty and delight. These children cleared out of the way and watched the boat go by with unwilling respect; they shouted questions after it, wanting to know where it came from and what was going to be done with it. No one answered them. Eva and Carol as well as the boys refused to answer or even look at them.

The five of them entered Clayton's yard. The boys shifted weight, as if they were going to put the boat down.

"You better take it round to the back where nobody can see it," Carol said. That was the first thing any of them had said since they came into town.

The boys said nothing but went on, following a mud path between Clayton's house and a leaning board fence. They let the boat down in the back yard.

"It's a stolen boat, you know," said Eva, mainly for the effect. "It must've belonged to somebody. You stole it."

"You was the ones who stole it then," Bud said, short of breath. "It was you seen it first."

"It was you took it."

"It was all of us then. If one of us gets in trouble then all of us does."

"Are you going to tell anybody on them?" said Carol as she and Eva rode home, along the streets which were dark between the lights now and potholed from winter.

"It's up to you. I won't if you won't."

"I won't if you won't."

They rode in silence, relinquishing something, but not discontented.

The board fence in Clayton's back yard had every so often a post which supported it, or tried to, and it was on these posts that Eva and Carol spent several evenings sitting, jauntily but not very comfortably. Or else they just leaned against the fence while the boys worked on the boat. During the first couple of evenings neighborhood children attracted by the sound of hammering tried to get into the yard to see what was going on, but Eva and Carol blocked their way.

"Who said you could come in here?"

"Just us can come in this yard."

74

These evenings were getting longer, the air milder. Skipping was starting on the sidewalks. Further along the street there was a row of hard maples that had been tapped. Children drank the sap as fast as it could drip into the buckets. The old man and woman who owned the trees, and who hoped to make syrup, came running out of the house making noises as if they were trying to scare away crows. Finally, every spring, the old man would come out on his porch and fire his shotgun into the air, and then the thieving would stop.

None of those working on the boat bothered about stealing sap, though all had done so last year.

The lumber to repair the boat was picked up here and there, along back lanes. At this time of year things were lying around — old boards and branches, sodden mitts, spoons flung out with the dishwater, lids of pudding pots that had been set in the snow to cool, all the debris that can sift through and survive winter. The tools came from Clayton's cellar — left over, presumably, from the time when his father was alive — and though they had nobody to advise them the boys seemed to figure out more or less the manner in which boats are built, or rebuilt. Frank was the one who showed up with diagrams from books and *Popular Mechanics* magazines. Clayton looked at these diagrams and listened to Frank read the instructions and then went ahead and decided in his own way what was to be done. Bud was best at sawing. Eva and Carol watched everything from the fence and offered criticism and thought up names. The names for the boat that they thought of were: Water Lily, Sea Horse, Flood Queen, and Caro-Eve, after them because they had found it. The boys did not say which, if any, of these names they found satisfactory.

The boat had to be tarred. Clayton heated up a pot of tar on the kitchen stove and brought it out and painted slowly, his thorough way, sitting astride the overturned boat. The other boys were sawing a board to make a new seat. As Clayton worked, the tar cooled and thickened so that finally he could not move the brush any more. He turned to Eva and held out the pot and said, "You can go in and heat this on the stove."

Eva took the pot and went up the back steps. The kitchen seemed black after outside, but it must be light enough to see in, because there was Clayton's mother standing at the ironing board, ironing. She did that for a living, took in wash and ironing.

"Please may I put the tar pot on the stove?" said Eva, who had been brought up to talk politely to parents, even wash-and-iron ladies, and who for some reason especially wanted to make a good impression on Clayton's mother.

"You'll have to poke up the fire then," said Clayton's mother, as if she doubted whether Eva would know how to do that. But Eva could see now, and she picked up the lid with the stove-lifter, and took the poker and poked up a flame. She stirred the tar as it softened. She felt privileged. Then and later. Before she went to sleep a picture of Clayton came to her mind; she saw him sitting astride the boat, tar-painting, with such concentration, delicacy, absorption. She thought of him speaking to her, out of his isolation, in such an ordinary peaceful taking-for-granted voice.

On the twenty-fourth of May, a school holiday in the middle of the week, the boat was carried out of town, a long way now, off the road over fields and fences that had been repaired, to where the river flowed between its normal banks. Eva and Carol, as well as the boys, took turns carrying it. It was launched in the water from a cow-trampled spot between willow bushes that were fresh out in leaf. The boys went first. They yelled with triumph when the boat did float, when it rode amazingly down the river current. The boat was painted black, and green inside, with yellow seats, and a strip of yellow all the way around the outside. There was no name on it, after all. The boys could not imagine that it needed any name to keep it separate from the other boats in the world.

76

Eva and Carol ran along the bank, carrying bags full of peanut-butter-and-jam sandwiches, pickles, bananas, chocolate cake, potato chips, graham crackers stuck together with corn syrup and five bottles of pop to be cooled in the river water. The bottles bumped against their legs. They yelled for a turn.

"If they don't let us they're bastards," Carol said, and they yelled together, "We found it! We found it!"

The boys did not answer, but after a while they brought the boat in, and Carol and Eva came crashing, panting down the bank.

"Does it leak?"

"It don't leak yet."

"We forgot a bailing can," wailed Carol, but nevertheless she got in, with Eva, and Frank pushed them off, crying, "Here's to a Watery Grave!"

And the thing about being in a boat was that it was not solidly bobbing, like a log, but was cupped in the water, so that riding in it was not like being on something in the water, but like being in the water itself. Soon they were all going out in the boat in mixed-up turns, two boys and a girl, two girls and a boy, a girl and a boy, until things were so confused it was impossible to tell whose turn came next, and nobody cared anyway. They went down the river — those who weren't riding, running along the bank to keep up. They passed under two bridges, one iron, one cement. Once they saw a big carp just resting, it seemed to smile at them, in the bridge-shaded water. They did not know how far they had gone on the river, but things had changed — the water had got shallower, and the land flatter. Across an open field they saw a building that looked like a house, abandoned. They dragged the boat up on the bank and tied it and set out across the field.

"That's the old station," Frank said. "That's Pedder Station." The others had heard this name but he was the one who knew, because his father was the station agent in town. He said that this was a station on a branch line that had been torn up, and that there had been a sawmill here, but a long time ago.

Inside the station it was dark, cool. All the windows were broken. Glass lay in shards and in fairly big pieces on the floor. They walked around finding the larger pieces of glass and tramping on them, smashing them, it was like cracking ice on puddles. Some partitions were still in place, you could see where the ticket window had been. There was a bench lying on its side. People had been here, it looked as if people came here all the time, though it was so far from anywhere. Beer bottles and pop bottles were lying around, also cigarette packages, gum and candy wrappers, the paper from a loaf of bread. The walls were covered with dim and fresh pencil and chalk writings and carved with knives.

I LOVE RONNIE COLES

KILROY WAS HERE

RONNIE COLES IS AN ASS-HOLE

WHAT ARE YOU DOING HERE?

WAITING FOR A TRAIN

DAWNA   MARY-LOU   BARBARA   JOANNE

It was exciting to be inside this large, dark, empty place, with the loud noise of breaking glass and their voices ringing back from the underside of the roof. They tipped the old beer bottles against their mouths. That reminded them that they were hungry and thirsty and they cleared a place in the middle of the floor and sat down and ate the lunch. They drank the pop just as it was, lukewarm. They ate everything there was and licked the smears of peanut butter and jam off the bread-paper in which the sandwiches had been wrapped.

They played Truth or Dare.

"I dare you to write on the wall, I am a Stupid Ass, and sign your name."

"Tell the truth — what is the worst lie you ever told?"

78

"Did you ever wet the bed?"

"Did you ever dream you were walking down the street without any clothes on?"

"I dare you to go outside and pee on the railway sign."

It was Frank who had to do that. They could not see him, even his back, but they knew he did it, they heard the hissing sound of his pee. They all sat still, amazed, unable to think of what the next dare would be.

"I dare everybody," said Frank from the doorway, "I dare — Everybody."

"What?"

"Take off all our clothes."

Eva and Carol screamed.

"Anybody who won't do it has to walk — has to *crawl* — around this floor on their hands and knees."

They were all quiet, till Eva said, almost complacently, "What first?"

"Shoes and socks."

"Then we have to go outside, there's too much glass here."

They pulled off their shoes and socks in the doorway, in the sudden blinding sun. The field before them was bright as water. They ran across where the tracks used to go.

"That's enough, that's enough," said Carol. "Watch out for thistles!"

"Tops! Everybody take off their tops!"

"I won't! We won't, will we, Eva?"

But Eva was whirling round and round in the sun where the track used to be. "I don't care, I don't care! Truth or Dare! Truth or Dare!"

She unbuttoned her blouse as she whirled, as if she didn't know what her hand was doing, she flung it off.

Carol took off hers. "I wouldn't have done it, if you hadn't!"

"Bottoms!"

Nobody said a word this time, they all bent and stripped themselves. Eva, naked first, started running across the field, and then all the others ran, all five of them running bare through the knee-high hot grass, running towards the river. Not caring now about being caught but in fact leaping and yelling to call attention themselves, if there was anybody to hear or see. They felt as if they were going to jump off a cliff and fly. They felt that something was happening to them different from anything that had happened before, and it had to do with the boat, the water, the sunlight, the dark ruined station, and each other. They thought of each other now hardly as names or people, but as echoing shrieks, reflections, all bold and white and loud and scandalous, and as fast as arrows. They went running without a break into the cold water and when it came almost to the tops of their legs they fell on it and swam. It stopped their noise. Silence, amazement, came over them in a rush. They dipped and floated and separated, sleek as mink.

Eva stood up in the water her hair dripping, water running down her face. She was waist deep. She stood on smooth stones, her feet fairly wide apart, water flowing between her legs. About a yard away from her Clayton also stood up, and they were blinking the water out of their eyes, looking at each other. Eva did not turn or try to hide; she was quivering from the cold of the water, but also with pride, shame, boldness, and exhilaration.

Clayton shook his head violently, as if he wanted to bang something out of it, then bent over and took a mouthful of river water. He stood up with his cheeks full and made a tight hole of his mouth and shot the water at her as if it was coming out of a hose, hitting her exactly, first one breast and then the other. Water from his mouth ran down her body. He hooted to see it, a loud self-conscious sound that nobody would have expected, from him. The others looked up from wherever they were in the water and closed in to see.

Eva crouched down and slid into the water, letting her head go right under. She swam, and when she let her head out, downstream, Carol was coming after her and the boys were already on the bank, already running into the grass, showing their skinny backs, their white, flat buttocks. They were laughing and saying things to each other but she couldn't hear, for the water in her ears.

"What did he do?" said Carol.

"Nothing."

They crept in to shore. "Let's stay in the bushes till they go," said Eva. "I hate them anyway. I really do. Don't you hate them?"

"Sure," said Carol, and they waited, not very long, until they heard the boys still noisy and excited coming down to the place a bit upriver where they had left the boat. They heard them jump in and start rowing.

"They've got all the hard part, going back," said Eva, hugging herself and shivering violently. "Who cares? Anyway. It never was our boat."

"What if they tell?" said Carol.

"We'll say it's all a lie."

Eva hadn't thought of this solution until she said it, but as soon as she did she felt almost light-hearted again. The ease and scornfulness of it did make them both giggle, and slapping themselves and splashing out of the water they set about developing one of those fits of laughter in which, as soon as one showed signs of exhaustion, the other would snort and start up again, and they would make helpless — soon genuinely helpless — faces at each other and bend over and grab themselves as if they had the worst pain.

LITTLE GIRLS
P. K. Page

More than discovery — rediscovery.
They renew
acquaintanceship with all things
as with flowers in dreams.

And delicate as a sketch made by being,
they merge in a singular way with their own thoughts,
drawing an arabesque with a spoon or fork
casually on the air behind their shoulders,
or talk in a confidential tone as if
their own ears held the hearing of another.

Legs in the dance go up as though on strings
pulled by their indifferent wanton hands

while anger blows into them and through
   their muslin
easily as sand or wind.

Older, they become round and hard, demand
shapes that are real, castles on the shore
and all the lines and angles of tradition
are mustered for them in their eagerness
to become whole, fit themselves to the thing
they see outside them,
while the thing they left
lies like a caul in some abandoned place,
unremembered by fingers or the incredibly
   bright
stones, which for a time replace their eyes.

YOUNG GIRLS

P. K. Page

Nothing, not even fear of punishment
can stop the giggle in a girl.
Oh mothers' trim
shapes on the chesterfield cannot dispel
their lolloping fatness.
Adolescence tumbles about in them
on cinder schoolyard or behind the expensive gates.

See them in class like porpoises
with smiles and tears
loosed from the same subterranean faucet; some
find individual adventure in
the obtuse angle, some in a phrase
that leaps like a smaller fish from a sea of words.
But most, deep in their daze, dawdle and roll,
their little breasts like wounds beneath their clothes.

A shoal of them in a room makes it a pool.
How can one teacher keep the water out,
or, being adult, find the springs and taps
of their tempers and tortures?
Who on a field filled with their female cries
can reel them in on a line of words
or land them neatly in a net?
On the dry ground they goggle, flounder, flap.

Too much weeping in them and unfamiliar blood
has set them perilously afloat.
Not divers these — but as if the waters rose in flood —
making them partially amphibious
and always drowning a little and hearing bells;
until the day the shore line wavers less,
and caught and swung on the bright hooks of their sex,
earth becomes home, their natural element.

A WOMAN IN POLITICS
Judy LaMarsh

Nothing was so hard to accomplish during all the time I was
in Cabinet as the appointment of a Royal Commission to
inquire into the Status of Women. Not long after I took
office, I broached the matter with the Prime Minister,
pointing out to him that President Kennedy had recognized
the signs of unrest among women of his own country and had
set up just such a commission. Although the Kennedy
Commission was disappointing in its report, partly because of
the federal state with conflicting jurisdictions, it did stimulate
similar inquiries in most of the states, and did ensure that
there would be a continuing interest in finding solutions to
expose inequalities. In early 1965, Pearson seemed at last to
be prepared to accept my advice and to set up such a
commission. I had provided him with a draft of the proposed
terms of reference, with a copy of the Kennedy Commission's
reference and its report, together with a long list of women
who might serve on such a commission.

When I mentioned a Royal Commission to a national
women's meeting, there was an immediate and scathing
reaction from some of the responsible press of the country.
Pearson backed off as if stung with a nettle. I had raised it
repeatedly over the years, but was put off with the explanation
that Premier Lesage had objected to such a commission
because it would impinge upon the jurisdiction of the
provinces. This may or may not be true, as an effective
commission must cross provincial boundaries, but I cannot see
how it is any more the case than that of the Bicultural and
Bilingual Commission. It seems odd to think that in some
men's minds women belong predominantly to the provinces. It
was my hope that such a commission might be set up to bring
in its report by 1967. In the event, it was set up in 1967,
hopefully to report in 1968, the International Human Rights
year. It should not be long delayed. It may not, as many
Royal Commissions have not, solve all the problems, but it
should provide an airing of women's complaints in a national

forum, and if it is solidly done many of its recommendations may be implemented. On the other hand, without anyone interested remaining in Government, it may well languish as have so many other Royal Commission Reports. There seems no one now within Government circles who is interested in seeing its recommendations take legislative form. It is, therefore, up to the women of the country to put on the pressure and keep it on.

I have no doubt in my own mind that I would have been unable to convince the Government to set up the commission without the remarkable organization of Mrs. Laura Sabia of St. Catharines, Ontario, who, for the first time in history, brought together women's organizations from all over the country to speak with one voice in Ottawa. That was the pressure needed to make Pearson act, so he finally conceded that he would set up the Commission. He sought suggestions for the names of the commissioners from me. I suggested as one of them Donald Gordon Jr., who saw women as people. As the chairman, there was a well-known woman in public affairs with fluent French, Mrs. Florence Bird (Anne Francis), and I thought her appointment would be well-received. Then there was Elsie Gregory MacGill, a consulting engineer from Toronto, whose mother had been one of the first of Canada's fighters for women's rights. I found Mrs. Lang from Alberta through the help of the farm organizations. I would have preferred the commissioners to include more single women and some younger ones, but I was content that at least it was appointed and off the ground. It has had much internal difficulty, and I do not believe its research is deep enough, nor has it been given sufficient time to be thorough, but it has attracted interest among enlightened people to the inequalities which now exist for women in Canadian life.

* * *

I grew tired of being the woman's watchdog. I grew tired of having the role thrust upon me simply because I was a woman. I was paid exactly what my male colleagues were paid, although many of them did not perform one-fifth of the work I did for the Government or for the Liberal Party. I was particularly bitter about a Supreme Court of Ontario judgment released in early 1968. The case involved a policewoman in Northern Ontario who was paid less than her colleagues because, as a woman, she did not perform the same duties as they, and also because she did not have the same dependants to provide for! In the words of Mr. Justice Fergusson, of that Court, this inequality conforms to "all the rules of civilization, economics, family life and common sense". This is Ontario, in 1968!

I was always expected to be present when we had women's delegations attending upon the Cabinet. I was, further, expected to be particularly diligent in attending conventions of the party's women, and to make regular rounds in speaking to any and every women's organization which proffered me an invitation. I was the usual invitee whenever any organization, anywhere in Canada, held its annual "ladies night". I was asked to fashion shows, award dinners, and meetings of the professions in which women were a dominant group. My clothes, my stockings, my wigs were a matter of public discussion. (Until Pierre Elliott Trudeau, I do not remember any other member's style of dressing ever discussed in the public print.) My weight, my age, my home, my cooking, my hobbies, my friends, my tastes, my likes and dislikes, all became public property to a degree suffered by none of my colleagues, including the Prime Minister. I was two or three times named "Woman of the Year" (not because of anything I did which was important, but because more lines of type appeared about me than about any other woman). Reporters followed me into the hairdresser's, photographers tagging along. Executive women followed me into washrooms, wives clustered about me in airports to receive me as I stumbled, bedraggled and exhausted, from an aircraft for yet another meeting. Children and teachers wrote me for recipes and for tips on how to get along as a woman. Columnists asked me about anything and everything — except about my job. Women's magazines and women's pages featured articles about me — sometimes without bothering to interview me. Cartoonists delighted in sketching me and my clothes and swelling girth. And always the whispers and speculation about my sex life — how much, and with whom? Every member with a pack of eager school-children visiting sought out the lady minister to talk to; every member with a group of women politicians in tow asked me to meet with them; every woman politician from another country who visited Ottawa was at once shown in to me. I could not shop without being recognized and spoken to, my purchases eyed, the prices I was paying assessed. I could not walk down the street in Ottawa, or elsewhere, without being constantly on parade. Although most of these encounters were pleasant, the curiosity of the public took the greatest toll of me of anything in politics. For a while I talked freely on television and to the press, hoping that once my views were thoroughly known, I would be an object of curiosity no longer, but the publicity seemed to increase it. When I was first elected to Parliament, I was approached by Gerald Waring, a columnist and reporter to my hometown newspaper. One of the first things he asked me, as we sat in the noisy madhouse of the parliamentary cafeteria, was, "Are you a politician, or a woman?" Just as though the two were mutually exclusive! And that inquisitiveness only reflected what others thought.

* * *

Women will someday be equal in Canada and elsewhere in the Western World. We have come from being chattels or wards in the last hundred-odd years. Through periods of incredible adversity as pioneer wives and daughters, we have filled the breach in every conceivable role when wars drain off manpower. Each year we inch closer to true equality of opportunity. If the French Canadians can make it, if the Negroes and Indians can make it, then it is likely that women will make it too.

Say it isn't so . . .

TRUCE

P. K. Page

My enemy in a purple hat
looks suddenly like a plum
and I am dumb with wonder
at the thought
of feuding with a fruit.

HOUSEWORK GIVES ME THE CRAZIES
Marian Engel

Quite a long time ago the suggestion came that I write an article on housekeeping. But each time I sat down to it, I have looked around my office, always the worst room in the house, and decided that I am a hypocrite to write about housekeeping, and ripped the paper out of the typewriter. It always contained a delicious description of my grandmother's housekeeping.

This morning I have looked around the house and decided that it can be left to its grotty self as long as I call the article: ON NOT HOUSEKEEPING. Which is what I actually do.

My grandmother's house: paneled wood in the halls, rainbow doorknobs, big dark oil paintings; living room like the set for a play — brown broadloom, Victorian settees, puckered satin cushions, miniature ancestors. Kitchen: tiled, like mine, all white, spotless — unlike mine. Upstairs (the sleepless child knows all the drawers), a linen cupboard stacked with ironed sheets and towels, a drawer of old dolls, and, in the top drawer of the spare-room chiffonier, light bulbs, a music box, and a plush wind-up bird, green and black.

All those drawers neat as pins. The bathroom containing white towels only — color was vulgar — though a green can of Dr. Sand's pine bathsalts matched the green soap and the six hexagons of green tile in the floor.

I inherited the plush wind-up bird and a soup tureen I had always coveted, and some boxes of miscellaneous stuff that mean more to me now than land on the moon. My sister and my cousins inherited the beautiful housekeeping. Who's better off? None of us, I think. We're just different.

The perfection of that house, with its scent of ashes-of-roses, has lived in our minds for a very long time. I try to keep the memory where it belongs — as a model of how it is possible to do things, and nothing more. I can't do what she did — an indefatigable little black-eyed woman born on a farm, one of ten children early instructed in the art of keeping the wilderness at bay. She worked fiercely, did everything beautifully, and though, by the time they were in their seventies, she and her husband were probably what is called well-off, she wasn't extravagant. She simply never bought anything nasty, and always took care of what she had.

I liked best, though, a side of her that only came out the last time I saw her, eighty-nine and frail with a nightcap on, and, certainly, a frilled flannel nightgown and a crocheted bed jacket. Sitting up in bed saying, "Why Marian, I'm reading *East Lynne* again. I find I don't care for it as much as I used to, when I was a girl. Now I find I much prefer Jane Austen."

After she died, I was touched to find in her miscellany a pamphlet on famous women writers.

I was never touched by her housekeeping. It was beautiful, all right, but whenever I moved I broke something or soiled something; I felt like an oaf in her house.

The house we moved into last summer is a lot like hers — though the paneling is imitation — and I'm glad she's not around to see my housekeeping. I know, I think, what she'd think of my scruffiness.

But it's more important what I think of it, isn't it?

I am haunted by it, and perpetually guilty and defiantly untidy, and sometimes rampantly unfair, and often evasive on the subject of housekeeping — and not — housekeeping. And I think, too, that I'm wrong. Like a lot of other people in this country, on the subject of housekeeping I'm stuck in the nineteenth century. And I think it's terribly important to women like me — now — to get past centuries out of our heads and start living.

My grandmother inhabits the history of housekeeping. She was born in Ontario in the 1870s, and trained to do things the way they did them in Northern Ireland in the early 1800s before they came out here. I think she always had help — those were the days of hired men and girls, when you learned perfection then in order to impose it.

I know a lot more, really, about my mother and

housekeeping. She, too, was a historic case — and still is, in her neat little house. But she worked to another system. As a schoolteacher's wife in the Depression she learned to do without those stacks of virginal towels and learned to like doing without them. She is by nature a minimalist. She owns as little as she can, and lives within the smallest practical space. I think her ideal home was the trailer we had when we were little, before anyone else had trailers. We had lyrical summers in it, and everything was practical and shipshape and life was lived to a routine. We wore brown shorts and T-shirts, or seersucker dresses, slept in sleeping bags, which were aired first thing every morning, and ate the fish my father caught, except on Fridays when the meat man came along the beach. She did everything when it had to be done, kept us spick and span, and managed to have time to do some things for herself. (She didn't work outside the house, though she had before she was married: women who were married didn't work in the Depression, and got out of the habit later.)

I think, now, that that was real twentieth-century living. Keeping possessions down to an absolute minimum, doing what you had to do well, not lumbering yourself with too much work, too many things.

Her system doesn't work for me. My husband and I are living testimony to the fact that rolling stones do in fact gather moss. And the moss is dusty. What to do about it?

A lot of the time I do nothing. Like Virginia Woolf, I have a wonderful gift for not seeing dust. Except when company comes, when I flutter and twitter and notice the horrors under the chesterfield, the cooky crumbs in the carving on the coffee table, and start making genteel apologies.

Sometimes, I get a cleaning woman, but that has its hazards.

First of all, it's expensive — and why shouldn't it be? But then once you get someone good, there's a whole day when you can't work — at least I can't, because I work at home and it's impossible to live in the abstract when someone is doing your own concrete dirty work in the next room. And it takes too long to clean up so you can get your money's worth out of her labor.

And the best one I ever had — she was terrific and made me realize that no matter how hard I'd work I would never be any good at housework at all, I couldn't work like her, I wasn't that sort of person — wanted me to keep her company all day. She didn't like silence. We parted by mutual consent.

Then I hired a firm of cleaners — a great rush of people who arrived at the door and went through the house like a hurricane. They were expensive and efficient, but like a great many people in Toronto now, all of the darker races. I felt terrible making them do my dirty work. I thought of England and how at first there were some charming West Indian accents saying "Mind the doors" on the subway, and later a whole servant class; everybody doing anything menial in London when I was there two years ago was brown — and sulky-looking. And no wonder. It's too easy to let a country slide into passing the worst jobs off on colored immigrants. So now I'm on my own again, and happier.

Sometimes, to console myself for my bad housekeeping, I buy a book about housekeeping. The last one I bought, though, was no better than the first. It was called *The Psychiatrist's Wife's Book of Housekeeping* or something like that, and I thought it would be funny (a lot of women make a good living by writing funny things about housekeeping) and good. It was funny.

It had a quiz at the front, asking you questions about how many rooms, how many children, with extra points for twins, which I like because I have some. I did the quiz and came out an excellent housekeeper (by lying about the fact that the top three rooms in this house are rented to a really good housekeeper) and laughed aloud. Then I went on to the body of the book.

She tried to tell me the psychological reasons why I'd rather clean out the magazine rack than polish my silver. Cripes, I gave my silver to my sister years ago.

Peg Bracken's *I Hate To Housekeep Book* tells you how to make your own javelle water.

Now, I may be a rotten housekeeper but I know what end is up. In 1973 you don't have to worry about silver unless you want to. And baby, you're out of your mind to make your own javelle water unless you have to or unless you get a kick out of it.

Me, I'd like to live in a French hotel with a good cheap restaurant.

We got married in England, though we met in Canada. We were in our late twenties and had other things than domesticity on our minds. We lived in a hotel room and both worked. A Swedish *au pair* girl with long red rubber gloves came in and mopped, and made the beds every morning.

Then somebody gave us a cat, so we moved to an artist's studio, which was so big and so dusty I couldn't make any headway with it at all. It was full of straw carpeting that shed if it wasn't watered every day. We kept forgetting. But we were mostly too busy to notice the housekeeping, and very happy.

It was when we went to live on the island of Cyprus that I found out about my housekeeping. There, having always eschewed modernity before, we were given a large modern apartment by a friendly printer. It was over his press, and unrentable because you had to get your sea legs to live in it. It was floored with some kind of polished stone, which floored me. Unless you washed it very, very often it looked awful.

There was a lovely old mud-brick building across the narrow street. The monks who owned it hired old women to tear it down. All summer, the mud sifted into our place. My husband kept looking at me to see if I noticed. I didn't — until company came.

We bought a lot of snails to eat and kept two — Elizabeth and Philip — for pets. Elizabeth disappeared and was found after the heat was over (it was 112 inside in the summer) on the handle of the mop.

We came back to Canada eight years ago. I have since then

always lived in old houses with large cracks in them, and hot-air systems that blow the dust around. And cockroaches, which were often attributed to my housekeeping. Strange my housekeeping doesn't breed them after the fumigators have been around, isn't it?

I've been teased for my housekeeping, and nagged as well. I've brought two kids up who were spitters — those babies who barf up half their feed on the rug when they burp — and now they're seven and just leave Lego and cutting paper around. I've raved, screamed, got fat and depressed about housekeeping — been thoroughly silly. The funny thing is, I've done a lot of things that don't need to be done, for no reason but vanity.

When we first came back home, I looked up a friend of a friend who was a friend of Brendan Behan's. I found her living in a grand house full of expensive things with a plastic holy-water font in the front hall (never trust anyone who doesn't have something like a plastic holy-water font in the front hall, some touch of home or humanity: otherwise it was all done by a decorator, and the housekeeper is afraid of her own taste) and I asked her, "What on earth did you think of Canada when you first came over?" She threw up her hands, "Ah," she said, "the waxed floors, the silver tea sets, I near died. I wanted to go home, but he said, if I went home he wouldn't ever send me a ticket back."

Ah, the waxed floors, the silver tea sets, the signs that we are nice ladies. Ah, the op-art paintings, the shag carpets (there's a new kind of rake in the hardware store for shag carpets; who's making money out of those?), the signs that we are With It. Who cares?

That's the point, isn't it? Housekeeping isn't hard if you know who it's for. Yourself? Your husband? Your children? If you haven't got that worked out, you're doing a lot of work for someone who might possibly never arrive. (I think my grandmother was keeping house for God. Who might drop in. But she was born in the 1870s, a period when they were heavy on the idea that God sees all, but hadn't chosen to remember that God forgives as well.)

Most husbands like to eat well, not get marks on their dark suits when they sit down, and have a bit of fun. A friend of mine who is the cleverest housekeeper I know said that her mother-in-law told her years ago that a man will scowl at a house if the five things that annoy him most — dirty ashtrays, perhaps, or crooked pictures or rumpled drapes — are not attended to. The rest he simply doesn't notice.

She's nearly right. My husband notices everything, he's that kind of person. But we've had that out. If it really bothers him, he does it himself, or helps with it, or puts it on the list of Five Things. He no longer expects me to be superhuman. I've left him alone the odd time to cope while I went off on a job, and he thinks I'm fabulously disorganized — just as he is — and he's resigned now to living in what is often unkindly described as a mess.

We don't put things away in our house. We mean to, but there are always at least twelve books in the bathroom, fifteen on the coffee table, and twenty-five on either side of the bed. Periodically, we try to put them — and everything else — away. Then we can't find them. So I get mad at the kids for filing their toys in the middle of the front hall, and then I have to laugh and forgive.

It would be easier, I think, if like my mother I was a minimalist. She comes down and says "Marian, the books! Why don't you go to the library?" I really think she doesn't believe in owning things. Whenever we turned our backs at home, our five best things went off to the Salvation Army. She had no back numbers of the *New York Review of Books* lying around looking tatty then, and she still doesn't, and my sister and I finally made her promise not to give the good old things to the Sally Ann when she housecleans. We give her edible Christmas presents. We own so much more than she does and spend a heck of a lot of our lives trying to put it away.

We own too many things, we do too much, she tells us. I think she's darn well right. I wash more than she ever would have dreamed of doing with a wringer-washer, because I haven't taught the kids how to keep clean (how can I, who wipe my hands on my jeans as I cook and don't wear aprons?) and don't know what to do with half-soiled clothes, so I wash them. I don't iron much, thank goodness, because I get tangled up in things, but I sew, because Mother gave me her old machine when the twins were born, and it saves a lot of money. I don't use phosphate detergents, because my wash doesn't go on the line and doesn't have to look whiter than anyone else's — you shouldn't either.

Should? Isn't that the great Canadian word, though? It's hassled me all my life, through school and Sunday School and a Baptist university, which I thought was about books and turned out to be about people hanging in your doorway saying Marian, you shouldn't hang around with those people who read so much, you should curl your hair. Should should should until you think you're going to die of it. I've just read a lovely essay by George Woodcock, who among Canadian writers is a citadel of clarity, in which he says Canadians fail completely to discriminate between sins and crimes, and isn't he right?

But there are other more worrying trends, because there is some kind of Parkinson's law — whenever you get rid of one job another crops up. Right now in Toronto there's the community-school-ecology movement and I'm finding it hard to get my head straight about that.

What this means for me is that I keep all my bottles and take them to a recycling place. Keep all my newspapers. Flatten all my cans. Make a compost heap. Turn up at my kids' school and help. Shop at a co-op.

This house has a pantry, which I think is wonderful. It's full of empty wine and Vichy water and Nescafé bottles. I don't drive and my husband never has time to take them to the recycling place.

There's only one place for the newspapers to go — in my office.

I can't get out of the habit of emptying the sink-strainer into cans. I feel guilty.

The rabbit was the greatest compost heap — you fed him the outside leaves of the lettuce, the carrot peelings and cleaned his cage into the flower-beds. We never ate an old vegetable while he was around. A dog got him. But I like making compost, and sadly enough, I was just becoming a good gardener when my editor stopped by and looked at me, horrified. "Is that why the book isn't done?" he asked.

I don't go to the school. I have come to the conclusion that I have no talent for little kids. They make me feel inferior, I make them feel inferior. I'd best stay away. I do shop at a co-op, which I feel is a privilege — if it didn't take a non-driver so much time.

I believe in recycling, in nourishment, in community involvement. But I am also a person who periodically receives money from the Canada Council to buy time to write with, and there seem to be few methods of buying time that are ecologically sound.

I guess the really sound thing to do would be to send the bottles to the recycling depot in a taxi — but I'm too Canadian for that.

So I struggle on. I've given up having people to the house who might disapprove of my housekeeping. If you look as if you want silver tea on a silver tray, good-by. I try to be political, but I don't canvass any more. I haven't time. If you want me to stump for you in an election, I'll stand outside a subway station shouting your name for two hours and handing out pamphlets, that's all. But maybe you won't be able to find me, because in order to get out of most of these moral binds and buy time I've bought a little house in the country.

My mother shook her head. "Just what you need. Two houses to keep."

I agreed with her at the time. The place was a bargain . . . a little house in a country village. I got it furnished, all-in, from an estate. Once I saw what I had bought, I went and was sick over the lovely valley it clings to the side of. It was so very shabby.

But we had Christmas up there this year, Christmas without a telephone. We don't know many people in the village but we have friends four miles away, and spend a lot of time with them. They're hooked on living in the country, they come in with their big boots and think we're first rate because we have hot water in the kitchen sink and they don't. (*They* have a bathtub, though.) They don't mind the four layers of ancient linoleum, though I rather do. We had a grand Christmas. I got a goose I had watched grow up, and stuffed it with apples and chestnuts and put it in the oven. I was going to take it to their place, about four, but at two they dropped over to ask what time we were coming over, and I looked in the oven: the goose was perfection. By four it would be a ruined, shrunken hulk. We sat down at the big table under my daughter's summer picture *Still Life With Flypaper* and ate the goose. It was the best goose since Dickens and we let the kids eat peanut butter sandwiches instead out of pure goodwill.

You get into the country, if you're a city person — if you're a country person maybe the city does this for you — and you are stripped of your pretensions, you are no longer wedged between the old puritanism and the new. Somehow, that old cloak of shouldness falls off. You know, suddenly; that you've been damn silly to apologize for not nursing your babies (I was so excited by having twins I didn't notice I didn't have milk until they asked me if I needed a pill to suppress it) and you realize, too, that you have to try to use your head and be sensible. Adelle Davis is all very well but she comes on so strong as a nutritional moralist that she makes my head swim with guilt. Besides, she's an American, and her nutritional morality was created by the American packaged food kick, which I never got into because I got married and started to cook in Europe.

When my first book came out, my husband took me down to New York, where I met, for the first time, my agent, who is elderly and Irish and charming. "What does a real writer do?" I asked him.

"What you want to do," he said firmly.

In my Canadian soul I was stunned. I had never been told such a heathen thing before.

Well, a housewife does what she wants to do, doesn't she? She can't do everything, she chooses an end product — or, if she is unlucky, accepts an end product that is forced upon her — and works toward it. I have moments of deluded grandeur when I want to live in Buckingham Palace but I'm too lazy to work toward that aim, and I read too much, and I think I'm right for me. After all, Lady Ottiline Morrell was a very grand dame indeed, sister of the Duke of Portland, and hostess to everybody who counted in England in the twenties, but when she went to Paris to meet the James Joyces, the only thing that struck her was the fact that they had their feet on the table. I'd rather have been James Joyce than a duke's sister by a long shot, so now I pretend that the city house is the country house, and do what I want. That entails a certain amount of housekeeping, but I don't bake my own bread and I'm finally old enough to know that as long as those pure white towels can't fold themselves and march into the linen closet, I won't have my grandmother's house, and feeling guilty about that is a great waste of time.

MEDITATIONS OF A SEAMSTRESS (1)
Gwendolyn MacEwen

When it's all too much to handle
and the green seams of the world start fraying,
I drink white wine and sew
like it was going out of style;
      curtains become dresses, dresses
become pillowcovers, clothes
I've worn forever get taken in or out.
Now I can't explain exactly
what comes over me, but when the phone rings
I tell people I'm indisposed;
I refuse to answer the door, I even
neglect my mail.
      (Something vital is at stake,
the Lost Stitch or the Ultimate Armhole,
I don't know what) and hour after hour
on the venerable Singer
I make strong strong seams for my dresses
and my world.
      The wine possesses me
and I sew like a fiend, forgetting to use
the right colours of thread, unable to make
a single straight line;
I know somehow I'm fighting time
and if it's not all done by nightfall
everything will come apart again;
continental shelves will slowly drift into the sea
and earthquakes will tear wide open
the worn-out patches of Asia.

Dusk, a dark needle, stabs the city
and I get visions of chasing fiery spools of thread
mile after mile over highways and fields
until I inhabit some place at the hem of the world
where all the long blue draperies
of skies and rivers wind;
      spiders' webs describe
the circling of their frail thoughts forever;
everything fits at last and someone has lined
the thin fabric of this life I wear with grass.

KILL DAY ON THE GOVERNMENT WHARF
Audrey Thomas

"I only wish," she said, refilling his coffee mug, "that it was all a little more primitive."

The man, intent on his fried bread and tomato, did not hear or chose to ignore the wistfulness in her voice. Mouth full, he chuckled, and then, swallowing, "all what?"

"All *this*," she said impatiently, gesturing towards the inside of the little cabin. They were sitting by the window, having breakfast. It was nine o'clock on a Sunday morning and the sky outside bulged and sagged with heavy bundles of dirty-looking clouds. He wanted to get back out on the water before it rained.

"I thought you liked it here," he said, challenging her with a smile. She was playing games again.

"I do. I love it. I really don't ever want to go back. But," she said, looking at him over the rim of her mug, "seeing that the old man died only a few months later, don't you think it was rather unkind of Fate to have suggested plumbing and electricity to him? I mean," she added with a smile, "also seeing as how we were going to be the reluctant beneficiaries of all that expense."

"You may be reluctant," he said, wiping his mouth, "I'm not. I think we were damned lucky myself."

She shrugged and stood up to clear the table, rubbing the small of her back unconsciously. She had acquired a slight tan in the ten days she'd been away and he thought how well she looked. There was a sprinkling of pale greeny-coppery freckles across her nose and along her arms. She looked strong and self-reliant and almost pretty as she stood by the window with the stacked plates in her hand. It was not a myth, he thought, or a white lie to make them feel better. Women really do look better when they're pregnant. Sometimes she would say to him, quite seriously,

"Tom, do you think I'm pretty?" or

"Tom, what would you say about me if you saw me across the room?"

Her questions made him impatient and embarrassed and he usually ended up by returning some smart remark because he was both a shy and a truthful man. He wished she would ask him now, but he did not volunteer his vision. Instead he got up and said,

"Where's Robert?"

"Right on the porch. I can see him. He has a dish full of oysters and clams and a hermit crab in a whelk shell. He's been fascinated by it for two days now. I didn't know," she added, "that barnacles were little creatures. They've got little hand-like things which come out and scoop the water, looking for food."

"Yes, I believe those are actually their feet," he said. "My grandfather told me that years ago. They stand on their heads, once they become fixed, and kick the food into their mouths for the rest of their lives. Now *that's* primitive for you." He drew on his pullover again. "How would you feel if I had another little fish-around before it rains? Then I'll take Robert for a walk and let you have some peace."

"Oh he's alright, except sometimes when he wants to crawl all over me. He's actually better here than at home. Everything excites him. He could live here forever as well."

"You must come back soon," he reminded her gently, "whether you like it or not."

"I don't want to. I hate the city. And I like it better now," she said, "than later on, when all the summer people come."

"You don't get lonely?"

"No, not at all." She was embarrassed to admit it and irritated he had asked. "I walk and sit and look and read my books at night or listen to the radio. And there's Robert of course. He's become afraid of the dark, though," she said thoughtfully, "I wonder why. He wakes me up at night."

"Weren't you?" he challenged. "I was."

She turned surprised. She had been of course, but she was a very nervous, sickly child. This big sturdy, competent man who seemed afraid of nothing!

"Yes," she stood at the sink, soapy hands held out of the water, poised over a plate, remembering. "I used to lie very still because I was absolutely sure there was someone in the room. If he knew I was awake, or if I should call out, he would strangle me or slit my throat."

"Footsteps on stairs," he said, rolling a cigarette.

"Faces outside windowpanes," she countered.

"And don't forget," he added, "the boy may actually have seen something. A deer, or even the Hoopers' dog. I've seen him stand up and pull that curtain back after his nap. Leave the light on." He put the tobacco tin back on the window sill and got up. "Leave the bathroom light on. It won't break us."

"Won't that make him weak?" she cried. "Isn't that giving in to his fears?"

"Not really. He'll outgrow it. I think maybe that kind of strength comes from reassurance." He kissed the back of her hair. "See you later on."

"Bring us back a fish," she said, reminding him of his role as provider, knowing in her heart it was all one to him whether he landed a fish or not. She was jealous of his relationship with the little boat, the oars, the sea. He would come back with a look of almost sensual pleasure on his face.

He went out, banging the door and she could hear him teasing the little boy, explaining something. She left the dishes to dry and poured herself another cup of coffee. The baby kicked and she patted her abdomen as though to reassure it. Boy or girl, dark or light, she wondered idly but not very earnestly. It was out of her hands, like the weather and the tides. But would she really like to have it out here, maybe alone, with Robert crying from the prison of his crib or huddled at the foot of her bed, marked and possibly maimed forever by the groaning and the blood. Robert had been quick, amazingly and blessedly quick for a first child; the doctor had told her this indicated a rapid labour for the second. In her own way she was shy, particularly about physical things. Could she really go along to old Mrs. Hooper's and ask for help, or accept the possibility of being taken off the island by one of the local fishing boats, observed by the taciturn, sun-baked faces of the men to whom she would be, if known at all, simply another one of the summer folk.

It was easier in the old days, she felt, when there were no choices. She smiled at herself, for Tom, if he had been listening, would have added "and childbed fever, and babies dying, and women worn out before they'd hardly begun." He called her a romantic and accused her of never thinking things through. *He* was the one who could really have survived here without complaint, in the old days. He was the one who had the strength to drag up driftwood from the little rocky beach, and saw it up by hand, and the knowledge which enabled him to mend things or to start a perfect fire every time. He hauled his little rowboat down to the wharf below their place on a triangular carrier he'd made from old wheels off a discarded pram, pulled it down the narrow ramp, which could be very steep when the tide was out, lowered it over the side, stepped in carefully and rowed away. She was jealous of his strength and his knowledge when he was around — he had grown up in the country and by the sea. She was a city girl and forever yearning after the names of things. She dreamed; he did. Her hands were terribly clumsy, except when loving her husband or her son and she often lamented that she had never learned to knit or weave or even to play an instrument. She liked to read and to walk and to talk and felt herself to be shallow and effete.

Yet since they had found the cabin she had experienced a certain degree of content and growing self-respect. She had learned to bake good, heavy bread in the little two burner hotplate/oven which she hoped to replace, eventually, with an old, iron wood- or oil-burning stove; she had learned about ammonia for wasp stings and how to recognize the edible mushrooms which grew in profusion near the abandoned school house. She could even light a fire, even if not a perfect fire, and almost every time.

She had bought a booklet on edible plants and was secretly learning something about the sustaining nature of the various weeds and plants which grew in profusion around her. She had started a herb garden in an old bureau drawer and already had visions of bunches of herbs drying from the kitchen ceiling, jars of rose-hip and blackberry jam, mushrooms keeping in brine in heavy earthenware crocks. Things could be learned from books and by experiment. She got a pencil and jotted down on a piece of drawing paper a list:

cod	thistles		pick salal
salmon	stinging nettles	?	maybe sell some of our apples,
oysters	blackberries	?	my bread
mussels	apples		
	mushrooms		
	dandelions		

plant a garden, make beer, ? a goat and chickens for Robert and the baby.

Then she laughed and crumpled up the paper and threw it in the pot-belly stove (her pride and joy and a present discovered for her by Tom) which heated the little kitchen. The fire was nearly out. She would set some bread and then take Robert down on the dock until Tom returned.

"Robbie," she called, knocking on the window, "d'you want to help me make bread?" From his expression she could tell he hadn't heard so she went to the other side of the room — Tom had knocked most of the wall out to make one big room out of two — and opened the front door. It was chilly and she shivered. "Hey, d'you want to help me make bread?"

He nodded, sturdy and solemn like his father, but with her light skin and hair. She undid his jacket and kissed him. His cheeks were very red.

"Your ears are cold," she laughed, holding his head, like a ball, between her hands. "And you smell like the sea. Where did you put your cap?"

"I dunno. I want some juice." He wriggled away from her and she thought with a stab of regret "So soon?" and tried to fix him as he was at just that moment, red-cheeked and fat, with his bird-bright eyes and cool, sea-smelling skin, to remember him like that forever.

"Come on," he said, tugging at her skirt, "juice and cookies."

"Who said anything about cookies?" she asked in mock severity.

"Juice," he repeated, quite sure of himself. "And two cookies. I'm allowed two cookies."

"Says who."

"Juice and two cookies," he said, climbing onto a chair by the kitchen table.

Afterwards, after they had smelled the yeast and kneaded the dough and made a tiny loaf for Robert in a muffin tin, she covered the bread and left it near the still-warm stove and took the child down on the wharf to watch the fishermen. There were three boats in, the *Trincomali*, the *Sutil*, and the *Mary T.* and they jostled one another in the slightly choppy water. She looked out towards the other islands for Tom, but couldn't see him. Then carefully she and the little boy went down the ramp to the lower dock, where most of the activity was taking place. A few of the Indians she knew by sight, had seen them along the road or in the little store which served that end of the Island; but most of the ten or so people on the dock or sitting on the decks of boats were strangers to her and she felt suddenly rather presumptuous about coming down at all, like some sightseer — which was, of course, exactly what she was.

"Do you mind if we come down," she called above the noise of the hysterical gulls and a radio which was blaring in one of the cabins. Two young men in identical red-plaid lumberjackets were drinking beer and taking a break on the dock of the *Mary T.* They looked up at her as she spoke, looked without curiosity, she felt, but simply recognizing her as a fact, like the gulls or the flapping fish, of their Sunday morning.

"Suit yourself Missus," said an older man who seemed to be in charge.

"But mind you don't slip on them boards."

She looked down. He was right, of course. The main part of
the lower dock was, by now, viscous and treacherous with
blood and the remains of fish gut. The men in their gumboots
stepped carefully. The kill had been going on for at least an
hour and the smell of fish and the cry of gulls hung thick in
the heavy air. There was an almost palpable curtain of smell
and sound and that, with the sight of the gasping fish, made
her dizzy for a moment, turned the wharf into an
old-fashioned wood-planked round-about such as she had clung
to, in parks, as a child, while she, the little boy, the Indians,
the gulls, the small-eyed, gasping fish, the grey and swollen
sky spun round and round in a cacophony of sound and smell
and pure sensation. She willed herself to stop, but felt slightly
sick — as she often had on the actual round-abouts of her
childhood — and buried her face in the sweet-smelling hair of
her child, as though he had been a posy. She breathed deeply,
sat up, and smiled. No one had seen — except perhaps the
two young Indians. Everyone else was busy. She smiled and
began to enjoy and register what she was seeing.

Everywhere there were fish in various stages of life or death.
Live cod swam beneath the decks of the little boats, round and
round, bumping into one another as though they were part of
some mad children's game, seeking desperately for a way out
to the open sea. Then one of the men, with a net, would
scoop up a fish, fling it onto the wharf where it would be
clubbed by another man, and disemboweled swiftly by a third,
the guts flung overboard to the raucous gulls. Often the fish
were not dead when they were gutted, she could see that, and
it should have mattered. The whole thing should have
mattered: the clubbing, the disembowelment, the sad stupid
faces of the cod with their receding chins and silly chinamen's
beards. Yet instead of bothering, it thrilled her, this strange
Sunday morning ritual of death and survival.

The fish were piled haphazardly in garbage cans, crammed
in, tails any old way, and carried up the ramp by two of the
men to be weighed on the scales at the top. The sole woman,

also Indian and quite young, her hair done up in curlers under a pale pink chiffon scarf, carefully wrote down the weights as they were called out. "Ninety-nine." "Seventy-eight." Hundreds of pounds of cod to be packed in ice until the truck came and took them to the city on the evening ferry boat. And at how much a pound, she wondered. Fish was expensive in the city — too expensive she thought — and wondered how much, in fact, went to these hard-working fishermen. But she dared not ask. Their faces, if not hostile, were closed to her, intent upon the task at hand. There was almost a rhythm to it, and although they did not sing, she felt the instinctual lift and drop and slice of the three who were actually responsible for the kill. If she had been a composer she could have written it down. One question from her and it might all be ruined. For a moment the sun slipped out, like a letter shoved under a heavy door, and she turned her face upwards feeling very happy and alive just to be there, on this particular morning, watching the hands of these fishermen, hands which glittered with scales, like mica, in the sunlight, listening to the thud of the fish, the creaking and wheeling of the gulls. A year ago she felt, the whole scene would have sickened her — now, in a strange way, she understood and was part of it. Crab-like, she could feel a new self forming underneath the old, brittle, shell — could feel herself expanding, breaking free. The child kicked, as though in recognition — a crab within a crab. If only Tom — But the living child tugged at her arm.

"I'm hungry."

"Ah, Robert. Wait a while." She was resentful. Sulky. He knew how to beat her.

"I want to pee. I want to pee *and* poop," he added defiantly.

She sighed. "O.K. you win. Let's go." She got up stiffly, from sitting in one position for so long. A cod's heart beat by itself just below the ramp. Carefully she avoided it, walking in a heavy dream up the now steeper ramp (the tide was going out already) and up the path to her cabin.

Still in a dream she cared for the child and wiped his bottom and punched the bread, turning the little oven on to heat. After the child had been given a sandwich she put him down for a nap and sat at the kitchen table, dreaming. The first few drops of rain began to fall but these she did not see. She saw Tom and a fishing boat and living out their lives together here away from the noise and terror of the city. Fish — and apples — and bread. Making love in the early morning, rising to love with the sun, the two of them — and Robert — and the baby. She put the bread in the oven, wishing now that Tom would come back so that she could talk to him.

"You only like the island," he had said, "because you know you can get off. Any time. You are playing at being a

primitive. Like still life of dead ducks or partridges or peonies with just one ant. Just let it be."

"What is wrong with wanting to be simple and uncluttered," she had cried.

"Nothing," he had replied, "if that is what you really are."

She began a pie, suddenly restless, when there was a knock on the door. It startled her and the baby kicked again.

"Hello," she said, too-conscious of her rolled-up sleeves and floury hands. "Can I help you?"

It was one of the young Indians.

"The fellows say you have a telephone, Missus. Could I use it? My brother-in-law wuz supposed to pick us up and he ain't come."

"Of course. It's right there." She retreated to the kitchen and sliced apples, trying not to listen. But of course there was no wall. Short of covering her ears there was little she could do.

"Hey. Thelma. Is that you Thelma? Well where the hell is Joe? Yeah. All morning. Naw. I'm calling from the house up above. Oh yeah? Well tell him to get the hell up here quick. Yeah. O.K. Be seeing you."

She heard the phone replaced and then he came around the big fireplace, which, with the pot-belly stove, divided the one large room partially into two. "Say," he said, "I got blood all over your phone. Have you got a rag?"

She looked at his hands, which were all scored with shallow cuts she could see, and the blood still bright orange-red and seeping.

"You're hurt."

"Naw," he said proudly, standing with his weight on one leg, "it's always like that when we do the cod. The knives is too sharp. *You* know," he added with a smile, as though she really did. Little drops of blood fell as he spoke, spattering on the linoleum floor.

"Don't you want some band-aids, at least?"

"Wouldn't last two minutes in that wet," he said, "but give me a rag to clean up the phone."

"I'll do it," she said, bending awkwardly to one of the bottom cupboards to get a floor cloth. She preceded him into the living room. He was right. The receiver was bright with blood, and some spots of blood decorated an air-letter, like notary's seals, which she had left open on the desk. Snow white in her paleness. He became Rose Red. What am I thinking of? She blushed.

"I sure am sorry," he said, looking at her with his dark bright eyes. "I didn't mean to mess up your things." She stood before him, the cloth bright with his blood, accepting his youth, his maleness, his arrogance. Her own pale blood drummed loudly in her ears.

"If you're positive you're all right," she managed.

"Yeah. Can't be helped. It'll all heal over by next Sunday." He held his hands out to her and she could see, along with the seeping blood, the thin white wire-like lines of a hundred former scars. Slowly she reached out and dipped two fingers in the blood, then raised them and drew them across her forehead and down across each cheek.

"Christ," he said softly, then took the clean end of the rag and spit on it and gently wiped her face. She was very conscious of her bigness and leaned slightly forward so he would not have to brush against her belly. What would *their* children have been like?

Then the spell broke and he laughed self-consciously and looked around.

"Sure is a nice place you've got here," but she was sure he didn't mean it. What would his ideal be? He was very handsome with his coarse dark hair and red-plaid lumberjacket.

"Well," she said, with her face too open, too revealing.

"Well," he answered, eager now to go. "Yeah. See you around. Thanks for the use of your phone."

She nodded and he was gone.

When Tom returned the little house was rich with the smells of bread and rhubarb pie and coffee.

"Any luck?"

"Yes," he said, "and no. I didn't catch anything — but you did."

"I did?" she said, genuinely puzzled.

"Yeah. One of the fishermen gave me this for you. He said you let him use the phone. It was very nice of him I must say."

And there, cleaned and filleted, presumably with the knife which had cut him so, was a beautiful bit of cod. She took it in her hands, felt the cool rasping texture of it, and wondered for an alien moment if his tongue would feel like that — cool, rough as a cat's tongue, tasting of fish.

"What did he say," she asked, her back to the man.

"He said 'give this to the Missus.' Why?"

"Nothing, I thought he was kind of cheeky. He made me feel old."

Later that night on their couch before the fire, she startled him by the violence of her love-making. He felt somehow she was trying to possess him, devour him, maybe even exorcise him. And why hadn't she cooked the cod for supper? She had said that all of a sudden she didn't feel like fish. He stared at her, asleep, her full mouth slightly open, and felt the sad and immeasurable gulf between them, then sat up for a moment and pulled the curtain back, looking vainly for the reassurance of the moon behind the beaded curtain of the rain. The man shook his head. There were no answers, only questions. One could only live and accept. He turned away from his wife and dove effortlessly into a deep, cool, dreamless sleep. The rain fell on the little cabin, and on the trees and on the government wharf below, where, with persistence, it washed away all traces of the cod and the kill, except for two beer bottles, which lolled against the pilings as the two young Indians had lolled so much earlier that day. The rain fell; the baby kicked. The woman moaned a little in her sleep and moved closer to the reassuring back of the puzzle who was her husband. And still the ageless rain fell on, and Sunday night — eventually — turned into Monday morning.

114

THE UNQUIET BED
Dorothy Livesay

The woman I am
is not what you see
I'm not just bones
and crockery

the woman I am
knew love and hate
hating the chains
that parents make

longing that love
might set men free
yet hold them fast
in loyalty

the woman I am
is not what you see
move over love
make room for me

IT'S THE STORY THAT COUNTS

Margaret Atwood

It's the story that counts. No use telling me this isn't a story, or not the same story. I know you've fulfilled everything you promised, you love me, we sleep till noon and we spend the rest of the day eating, the food is superb, I don't deny that. But I worry about the future. In the story the boat disappears one day over the horizon, just disappears, and it doesn't say what happens then. On the island that is. It's the animals I'm afraid of, they weren't part of the bargain, in fact you didn't mention them, they may transform themselves back into men. Am I really immortal, does the sun care, when you leave will you give me back the words? Don't evade, don't pretend you won't leave after all: you leave in the story and the story is ruthless.

QUESTIONS ON THE THEME:
The Role of Woman in Canadian Literature

1. Compare the problems identified by Marian Engel and Judy LaMarsh. What do they have in common?

2. Several of the selections deal with the development of self-awareness, e.g., "The Found Boat", "To Set Our House in Order", and "Christmas in Manitoba". How are they alike? In which of their concerns are they different?

3. While most of the material in the book reflects Canadian middle-class attitudes, there are exceptions. How do works such as "The Grey Archway", "Why Should I Care About the World", "I'm Sorry Mrs. Strauss", and "Canoe" reflect other cultures and life styles?

4. Many of the poems deal with a sense of being restrained. What are the restraints encountered by the speakers in "Jewellery", "The Mad Woman", and "The Lean Girl"?

5. Some writers reflect directly on their experiences as artists. What insights are provided by works such as "The Three Emily's", "Canoe", and "It's the Story That Counts"? How does "Real Women in Fiction, Where Are You?" deal with the problem?

6. Form often determines the statement of a work. Referring to selections in the anthology, show how the form of the editorial, magazine article, and short story affects the material in each.

7. Show how "Confidences" and "Kill Day on the Government Wharf" reflect the periods in which they were written.

8. Choose at least four selections in the book and discuss what aspects of being Canadian intrude on the consciousness of the writers.

9. What similarities can you find in "From a Dead Poet's Notebook" and "Springtime"?

BIBLIOGRAPHY

BIOGRAPHICAL INFORMATION

Carl F. Klinck, *A Literary History of Canada: Canadian Literature in English*, University of Toronto Press

Norah Story, *The Oxford Companion to Canadian History and Literature*, Oxford University Press

William Stewart Wallace, *The Macmillan Dictionary of Canadian Biography*, Macmillan of Canada

FICTION

Margaret Atwood, *The Edible Woman* and *Surfacing*, McClelland & Stewart

Marie-Claire Blais, *Mad Shadows*, New Canadian Library

Frances Moore Brooke, *The History of Emily Montague*, New Canadian Library

Marian Engel, *The Honeyman Festival*, Anansi

Anne Hébert, *Kamouraska*, Musson; *The Torrent*, Harvest House

Margaret Laurence, *The Diviners*, McClelland & Stewart; *The Fire Dwellers*, New Canadian Library; *A Jest of God*, McClelland & Stewart

Alice Munro, *Lives of Girls and Women* and *Something I've Been Meaning To Tell You*, McGraw-Hill Ryerson

Gabrielle Roy, *The Tin Flute*, New Canadian Library

Sheila Watson, *The Double Hook*, New Canadian Library

Ethel Wilson, *Mrs. Golightly and Other Stories* and *The Swamp Angel*, Macmillan of Canada

AUTOBIOGRAPHY

Emily Carr, *The Book of Small* and *The House of All Sorts*, Clarke, Irwin

Claire Martin, *In an Iron Glove*, McGraw-Hill Ryerson

Nellie L. McClung, *Clearing in the West: My Own Story*, Allen

L. M. Montgomery, *The Alpine Path: The Story of My Career*, Fitzhenry & Whiteside

POETRY

Margaret Atwood, *The Journals of Susanna Moodie*, Oxford University Press

Elizabeth Brewster, *In Search of Eros*, Clarke, Irwin

Gail Fox, *Dangerous Season*, Quarry Press

Phyllis Gotlieb, *Dr. Umlaut's Earthly Kingdom and Other Poems*, Calliope Press

Dorothy Livesay, *Collected Poems: Two Seasons*, McGraw-Hill Ryerson

Gwendolyn MacEwen, *The Armies of the Moon*, Macmillan of Canada

P. K. Page, *Poems Selected and New*, Anansi

Miriam Waddington, *Driving Home: Poems New and Selected*, Oxford University Press

AUDIOTAPES

Margaret Atwood, *The Twist of Feeling*, CBC Learning Systems

Annette Kolodny, *Devil Women*, CBC Learning Systems

Judy LaMarsh, *Interview*, OISE Political Materials

Margaret Laurence, in the *Canadian Writers Series*, OISE Publications

Dorothy Livesay, Gwendolyn MacEwen, and Miriam Waddington, in the *Canadian Poets Series*, OISE Publications

RECORDS

Margaret Atwood, narrated by Mia Anderson, *The Journals of Susanna Moodie*, CBC Learning Systems

Margaret Avison, Jay Macpherson, and Anne Wilkinson, on *Six Toronto Poets*, Folkways FL9806

Gwendolyn MacEwen and Phyllis Webb, on *Canadian Poets I*, CBC Learning Systems

FILMS

The following films are all available from the National Film Board.

Susan Gibbard, director, *Girls of Mountain Street*, colour, 10 min.

Joan Henson, director, *Three Guesses*, colour, 29 min.; *Standing Buffalo*, colour, 23 min.

Rhoda Leyer, director, *Little Red Riding Hood*, colour, 6 min.

Kathleen Shannon, director, *Like the Trees*, colour, 15 min.; *Luckily I Need Little Sleep*, colour, 8 min.

Clarinda Warny, director, *Happiness Is*, colour, 8 min.

Patricia Watson, director, *The Purse*, black & white, 12 min.; *The Summer We Moved to Elm Street*, colour, 28 min.

(Note: See also the National Film Board catalogue, *Projecting Women*, for titles that are in production by women film-makers.)

MAGAZINES

Branching Out, published monthly by Branching Out, Box 4098, Edmonton, Alberta

Magazines such as *Canadian Forum* frequently introduce new writing.

Women writers contribute regularly to *Chatelaine*, *Saturday Night*, and *Canadian Literature*.

57 67 77 87 97 08 18 28 38 48 THB 9 8 7 6 5 4 3 2 1